Library of Congress Cataloguing in Publication Data
Lee, Marshall M., 1945 —
A Passion for Quality.
 The First Fifty-Five Years of Electro Scientific Industries, 1944–1999
 p. 120
 Illustrated

1. History, Pacific Northwest
2. Business and Economics
3. Science
4. Technology

Electro Scientific Industries
Portland, Oregon
1999

ISBN 0-9674538-0-1

Photo Credits — Unless otherwise noted, all photos come from the ESI historical archives.
 Cover photography: Wayne Aldridge — West Linn, Oregon
 Photos courtesy of California Institute of Technology: p.1, p.2, p.8.
 Photos courtesy of Lawrence "Rocky" Rockwood: p.5, p.7.
 Photos courtesy of Oregon Historical Society: p.9, p.14, p.15.
 Photo courtesy of Douglas C. Strain: p.10.
 Photos courtesy of Larry Rapp: p.61, p.100.

Graphic Design & Print Management: Barnebey & Owen — West Linn, Oregon

Printing: Graphic Arts Center — Portland, Oregon

Book Binding: Lincoln & Allen — Portland, Oregon

To my friends at ESI,

Life holds countless twists and turns of fate, only a minute fraction of which we are conscious. In our conversations, Marsh Lee and I touched on those moments in my life, and in the life of Electro Scientific Industries, when history seemed to take its remarkable course. Who knew that in the fall of 1941, Rocky, Merle and I would meet at Cal Tech, much less join forces a decade later at ESI? What remarkable good fortune landed me in Portland in the fall of 1944, working with Harold Lawson in the Forest Service Radio Lab and with Frank Brown in his little sub-contracting operation making resistance bridges for General Radio? Although I knew that some day I might like to run my own company, I had no idea it would happen as soon as it did. And how lucky for me and for the company that I could talk my father, Clayton Strain, into joining me in the business! I've been so fortunate to be surrounded by such wonderful partners, associates and co-workers. Without them, the fire might have wiped us out. These remarkable people have been the inspiration and the source of our success in laser systems; they have seen us through bad times and the good.

A Passion for Quality captures those moments. It captures the mood and the spirit of the company I have so dearly loved and of which I am so deeply proud. And while I am intensely proud of the products ESI has made over the years, and of the service we have provided our customers, it is of the ESI family that I am most especially proud. As Professor Lee has made so abundantly clear, ESI's history is the story of our people and our culture. As I read these pages and look back on our fifty-five years together, I am reminded of the dignity of our work, the honor in serving the community, and the privilege of having been a member of the ESI family.

[signature]

Douglas C. Strain

It is with a sense of great satisfaction that today at ESI we can reflect on our past. In looking back, we can take comfort in the strength of those who saw the company through some of its most trying days. The fellowship and the bonds that held the ESI family together through fire, through death, through very difficult times, both move and inspire us as together we face the challenges of emerging markets and changing technologies. The company that began in 1944 with the Brown Bridge and blossomed into a world-class competitor, continues to be known for its leading edge technologies and its ability to partner with customers to develop creative solutions.

As we have grown, it has been impossible to retain the intimate scale of those early days. But what we demonstrate on a daily basis is that the new ESI of the 1990's can respond quickly, and with perhaps even greater agility than our smaller earlier incarnations. Without a doubt, new techniques and new business strategies have made this possible. And yet these new initiatives happen within the context of older values. The ESI story is thus one of continuity and change. The remarkable changes that we have seen during the past seven years, changes that required commitment and sacrifice on all our parts, these changes have their foundations firmly rooted in the continuity of those underlying values so lovingly voiced by Doug Strain, and captured so well in the following pages by Marsh Lee. As Marsh says in his introduction, this is an interpretation. Some will see things differently. So read on, and let the discussion begin!

[signature]

Don VanLuvanee

This project began in the spring of 1998, when Don VanLuvanee, Joe Reinhart and Larry Rapp approached me to inquire what a history of ESI might entail. The recent death of Merle Morgan, one of the company's "founding fathers," and the fact that ESI had reached its half-century mark, combined to create a sense that the time was right to capture ESI's past in a book. ESI had recovered from the near-fatal early-90's, its survival the result of a wonderful combination of strategic thinking, basic engineering and cutting-edge technology. And while the ESI of 1999 is hardly the ESI of 1979, much less the Electro-Measurements or Brown Engineering of even earlier days, the continuities within the fabric of ESI's culture are powerful and unmistakable. How to chronicle its past, capture its culture, and celebrate its accomplishments? This is where the historian comes in.

The historian's work is making sense out of the otherwise chaotic details of what companies invariably call their "stuff;" what historians refer to as documents, sources, evidence. And ESI had plenty of stuff, just as Larry promised. Thus, the first stage of the project was to inventory and archive ESI's historical collection. Equally important, however, is the oral history of an institution. Interviews with those who lived through ESI's past are an essential facet of this project, since the written record of a company must be augmented by eye-witness testimony. It is through their recollections that those who made the company can bring the past alive.

But what if there are contradictions between the written record and the oral recollections of employees, or worse, within the written evidence itself? The professional historian brings to bear aspects of the craft to resolve differences from among a variety of sources, to unravel complex events that unfold over years, to weigh cause and effect, and to look back over the entire life the company. While companies must focus on their future, seen in quarters, or annual cycles, the historian has the luxury of looking through a different lens.

The historian deals with facts, is trained to weigh the facts, and to offer an interpretation of those facts. *A Passion for Quality* focuses on the combination of people, technology and circumstance that form the first fifty-five years of ESI, from 1944 to 1999. Those seeking a complete inventory of every product ever made by ESI, or a listing of every employee ever to have drawn a paycheck from the company, will have to look elsewhere. What follows, then, is an interpretation. And since it is an interpretation, it is subject to question. To those who lived some, or all, of ESI's last fifty-five years, what follows may not always seem quite right. There may be things with which to quarrel, and this is good, for it stimulates conversation and debate, from which we can all benefit. But consider this: to the single soldier on the beach, the chaos of battle is intensely personal, as local and intimate as his survival. At a different extreme, to the general, the grander sweep of the battle takes on a completely different character. And years later, in the hands of the historian, the individual soldier, the general and the grand strategy are all woven together into a coherent story. Nevertheless, each individual soldier and each general will remember his own war somewhat differently. In these pages I have tried to honor the parts played by soldiers and generals, allowing to the greatest extent possible their voices to tell the story.

And what a story it is! The history of ESI did not happen in a vacuum. Just as American society emerged profoundly changed from World War II, so, too, did the young men who founded this company. During the past fifty-five years American society has become more open, yet more specialized, wealthier yet more competitive. Throughout, Americans faced triumph and tragedy, emerging from the Cold War victorious, but not without the scars of foreign war and political scandal. The history of ESI closely parallels these events.

Born out of the Second World War, modern electronics companies such as ESI mirrored the more open post-war American social structure. In the last half century the dizzying speed of technological change in America was facilitated by the electronics industry; and ESI was a critical part. Just as the changes in American society in the last fifty years have left their mark, at ESI the changes from measurement to lasers, and more recently on to vision and drilling, have not always come easily. ESI has remade itself many times over. Even before it was ESI, Doug Strain's arrival at Brown Engineering transformed the company into Brown Electro-Measurement Company. In 1953, BECO became Electro-Measurements, Inc., but not without crisis. Then, on the eve of its transformation into ESI, Electro-Measurements was gutted by fire. From the ashes on Macadam Avenue, a new company emerged: Electro Scientific Industries. With teamwork and sacrifice, ESI maintained its leadership in precision test and calibration equipment, while exploring new opportunities in electron microscopy and analog computing. By the end of the 1960's, however, a new technology beckoned: lasers. Once again, ESI would remake itself, emerging by the early 1980's as the leader in laser trimming and memory repair. Yet even as ESI went public, tragedy loomed; less than a year later, in 1984, the company lost its leader, Paul Lintner. In the following decade, buffeted by a prolonged cyclical downturn in the electronics industry, ESI struggled. By the mid-1990's, under the leadership of Board Chairman Dave Bolender and President/CEO Don VanLuvanee, ESI remade itself yet again. From its lowest point in 1992 a new ESI has emerged, reasserting its leadership in its core laser trimming and memory repair business, while establishing leading linkages to new technologies in vision, handling, packaging and drilling.

For fifty-five years, through ESI's doors have emerged instruments and systems known the world over for their precision. ESI's bridges set the standard. ESI's laser systems outperformed all comers. ESI's via Drill works at a micron level hitherto undreamed-of. The commitment to precision and excellence began at the top with Doug Strain and those who chose to join him. It continues to this day, woven inextricably into the fabric of ESI, its glistening thread reads: *A Passion for Quality*.

* * * * *

No project such as this is the result of one person's effort alone. And in true ESI fashion, this history is the product of many people pitching in to make things happen. Everywhere I went throughout the company I was met with enthusiastic support, a genuine willingness to help, and a generosity of spirit that has characterized the company from its earliest days. Along the way I have made many friends.

I am indeed grateful for the enthusiastic encouragement of Don VanLuvanee, President of ESI. From the very outset, Don's active interest in the project made my job a pleasure. In my career as a corporate historian I have been fortunate to have worked with presidents and board chairmen who have embraced the contribution that an historian can make to the culture of a company. The support of Don, and Dave Bolender, Chairman of ESI's Board of Directors, assured that my good fortune would continue unbroken. From day to day, the energy for the project came from Joe Reinhart, Vice President and Corporate Secretary, whose ability to get to the heart of the matter in whatever he engages makes him a particularly effective partner in any project one contemplates. Larry Rapp, Vice President, facilitated numerous arrangements and shared his voluminous knowledge of ESI on many occasions. Special thanks go to Larry for his willingness to help with the archiving of ESI's historical materials, and on a more personal note, for granting me the experience of working in T-1.

Of singular importance to my work was the cooperation of Douglas C. Strain, founder of ESI, and its first President and Chairman of the Board. Doug's willingness, indeed eagerness, to participate in the history project has made an incalculable contribution to my efforts. All those at ESI will certainly recognize the pleasure I had in interviewing Doug and in the many lengthy conversations he and I shared. Regardless of the topic or the lateness of the hour, and in the face of my often ignorant and naïve questions, we would end up doubled over in laughter, as Doug's infectious, mischievous wit inhabited every aspect of our conversations.

The sheer volume of scheduling and logistical details can often overwhelm the visiting historian. At ESI this never happened, since I knew even on short notice I could rely on the generous assistance of a number of key people. My thanks to Heather Grant and Toni Crites for their assistance, to Wendy Stallman, Sheri Bobzien, Kimberly McAlear, and Darlene Liebham and the staff of ESI's Corporate Communications Department for all their help, to Rhonda Reger and the entire crew in Facilities, especially John Holbrook and Dallas Buckman, for all their help with my office and materials arrangements. To Bonnie McCallum, head of ESI's Corporate Information Center, a special thanks for all her specialized assistance.

In the course of this project, many people made themselves available to me for interviews, often inconveniencing themselves to accommodate my schedule. The history of ESI is the history of the people who made – and continue to make – ESI such a success. I deeply appreciate their help, since their participation enriched the fabric of ESI's story. Foremost, of course, was Doug Strain. Essential were the recollections Lawrence "Rocky" Rockwood, Charlie Davis, and Armen Grossenbacher, all early key employees, and Ed Swenson. Others at ESI, past and present, to whom I owe a debt of gratitude are: Chris Beeler, Don Cutler, Karen Davies, Mike Ellsworth, Dean Finley, Dick Harris, Barry Harmon, Yolanda "Lonnie" Hermance, John McClosky, Bob Pailthorpe, David Pelinka, Larry Rapp, Joe Reinhart, Don Smith, Hollis Smith, Joan Sulman, Yun Long Sun, Joanne Sunnarborg, Steve Supalla, Don VanLuvanee, Gerda Woods, and Erwin Zander; present and past ESI Board members: Dave Bolender, John Elorriaga, Larry Hansen, Arthur Porter, Ralph Shaw, and William Walker.

At Pacific University, special thanks to Dean Tom Beck for his support, and to Connie Taylor for access to the material in the Strain Science Center; at the Oregon Historical Society, Steven Hallberg and Mikki Tint for their assistance with photos.

It is one thing to research and write a history; it is another to complete its publication. No list of acknowledgements would be complete, therefore, without thanking Ted Owen and Kathleen Barnebey of Barnebey & Owen, for their technical assistance in design and layout, and Wayne Aldridge whose photography graces the cover.

As always, it has been my intent to remain faithful not only to the words of my sources, but to their spirit as well. For whatever life and color inhabit these pages, they are responsible. For whatever errors in judgement may lie within, the fault is mine.

Finally, as with every project I undertake, the fruition of my labor results chiefly from the support of my wife, Esther Odiorne Lee. And, as ever, a simple thanks will not suffice.

Portland, Oregon
September, 1999

FOUR YOUNG MEN 1919-1944

The California Institute of Technology, in Pasadena, California, in the late 1930's

The "Three Horsemen" at Cal Tech

As fall yields to December in Pasadena, bright days and cool evenings embrace the well-tended gardens and palm-lined streets surrounding Cal Tech. Founded in 1891 as the Throop Polytechnic Institute, and changed in 1919 to the California Institute of Technology, Cal Tech is one of a handful of America's leading scientific colleges. As such, it gives off, as indeed does Southern California itself, an air of relaxed luxury. Nestled on the campus, a large rectangle of Spanish mission-style buildings, on the southeastern-most corner, is the Athenaeum, gathering place for faculty and guests. And on its walls hang the portraits of Cal Tech's 25 Nobel laureates. To study with one such man is honor enough, to have a faculty of present and future laureates is a priceless gift. Thus have generations of students been drawn to Pasadena and by 1941, tempered by the Great Depression, Cal Tech's student body worked with six present or future Nobel Prize winners. Three of those students – Douglas C. Strain, Merle S. Morgan, and Lawrence R. Rockwood – had unknowingly embarked on a course that would ultimately bring them together in Portland, Oregon, and that would lead to the creation of one of the world's leading high technology companies: Electro Scientific Industries.

All three young men – Strain, Morgan and Rockwood – had reached a similar point of entry to Cal Tech: junior year entry by examination. Cal Tech administered comprehensive examinations at the end of the sophomore year, producing a handful of vacancies each year. To fill these vacancies the school offered a competitive examination, open to all comers, that would allow some 30 students a year to transfer to Cal Tech at the beginning of the junior year. By far the greatest number of these junior transfers came from Pasadena Junior College, whose science faculty took great pride in placing so many of their students at their prestigious sister institution. "It was a great school," remembered Strain. "They had several professors of engineering who had been kicked out of Cal Tech for being too tough, believe it or not." Both Doug Strain and Lawrence Rockwood came from PJC, whose tuition-free education Rockwood recalled as arguably one of the nation's great bargains, while Merle Morgan won his transfer as a student at Fullerton Junior College in neighboring Orange County. "So," Doug Strain points out, "three of the Four Horsemen [who founded ESI] all got together at Cal Tech off and on over the next seven years."

The first days of December were particularly pleasant in 1941, as Cal Tech's students prepared for finals and the end of the term. And yet, intruding on the cloistered routine of students throughout the United States were the distant sounds of war, both in Europe and the Far East. Since June of that year Americans had followed the victorious progress of Germany's advance into Russia, while in the Far East American diplomacy sought vainly to retard Japan's conquest of China and Southeast Asia. Although still at peace, signs were everywhere that America was girding for war; in southern California those signs were especially clear, as Lockeed, Chance-Vaught, Republic, Grumman, and a host of smaller defense industries first moved from one shift to two, and ultimately to around-the-clock production.

For students at Cal Tech, preparations for war had already come close to home; many of their professors had for some time begun work on defense-related projects, in particular the physicist and Nobel laureate, Robert A. Millikan. "You could feel it in the air," recalled Doug Strain, "electronics and aircraft companies spun off projects. You could see it that fall in the lab. Cal Tech was actually very militaristic at the time." For many students this no doubt proved exciting, but for Doug Strain and Merle Morgan, the news that broke on Sunday, December 7, 1941, was sad indeed. Within hours of the Japanese attack on Pearl Harbor, National Guard troops arrived to secure the laboratories and scientific work on the Cal Tech campus. At 9:00 am the next morning, Monday December 8, students gathered in Culbertson Hall for a rally led by several administrators. Some students clamored to enlist; others wondered about their student deferments; Chemistry Professor and future Nobel laureate Linus Pauling appealed for calm, for reason to prevail.

Immediately following the rally, Doug and Merle were each summoned separately to the office of the Registrar. "I see you are registered 4E," was the greeting. Indeed, both young men were registered as conscientious objectors, a status made possible by the work after World War I of the Quakers and the Mennonite Brethren. "I recognize that you may have some claim to an educational deferment, but we have our own rules around here, and the rule is that you have to join the ROTC and take their oath... or you go." As Quakers, neither Doug nor Merle chose to take the oath. Could they finish the term? The answer was, "No." Leaving the Registrar's office, Strain went directly to Linus Pauling, whose intercession won both Strain and Morgan the right to take their exams and finish out the term. But by January both young men were out of school and on their way to four years of alternative service. Lawrence Rockwood, whose student deferment lasted until graduation in 1943, soon enlisted in the Navy, putting his engineering back-

Linus Pauling, in his office at Cal Tech, to whom Doug Strain and Merle Morgan turned in the days after Pearl Harbor for support as conscientious objectors. It was Pauling who made sure the two young men were allowed to finish out their semester before leaving for alternative service.

ground to good use in radar and sonar work for the duration of the war. Thus, the three lives that had briefly crossed on the Cal Tech campus in the fall of 1941 were torn apart by war. It was the war, however, that would shape each of the three young men — as well as the fourth of Doug's "Four Horsemen" Charlie Davis — each preparing to play his crucial role in the development of their company.

Doug Strain's evocation of the "Four Horsemen" recalls not the apocalyptic Biblical image of war, pestilence, famine and plague, but rather the four teammates of the Four Horsemen of Notre Dame, immortalized by the great sportswriter Grantland Rice in 1924. While all four worked together to accomplish more than any one of them could alone, quarterback Harry Stuhldreher remained Notre Dame's leader. So, too, from among ESI's Four Horsemen, one man stood out from the beginning as the leader: Douglas C. Strain.

Electrons and Radios

When Doug Strain talks about his childhood, his mind soon turns to his Scottish grandmother, Cora Linn Crockatt. She embodied the missionary zeal and background of his maternal ancestors, who in the late 19th Century settled in the Pacific Northwest to bring the word of the Disciples of Christ from Scotland to frontier natives, whether Indian or white. Similarly, Strain's paternal ancestors arrived by mid-century, fleeing famine and a bleak future in Ireland. The Strain family settled in Aurora, Oregon, where his grandmother was a school teacher for the Aurora religious community. Eventually the Crockatts settled in Pendleton, opening a church, where their mission was only modestly successful. The Crockatts moved to Spokane, but not before their daughter Edith completed high school in Pendleton. It was at Pendleton High School that Edith Crockatt met young Clayton Strain.

Edith and Clayton graduated together from Pendleton High School in 1911. In what was doubtlessly unusual for their day and age, both set out that fall to enroll as students at Oregon Agricultural College (later Oregon State University), Edith in home economics and Clayton in dairy husbandry. Graduating in 1915, they married and began managing a family farm in Idaho. Along with the farm, Clayton took on additional responsibilities as a county extension agent working on rodent control. Thus, when war came in 1917, despite his ROTC training as an Oregon Aggie, Clayton's government work exempted him from the draft. When, in 1919, the birth of their first child approached, the Strains dispatched Edith to Spokane to stay with her sister Helen, where, on October 24, 1919, Edith delivered a son, Douglas Campbell Strain.

The household into which the infant Douglas arrived was a relatively prosperous one. Clayton's farming was augmented by additional government work as county auditor and assessor and in 1927 Clayton moved his family to Gooding, Idaho, where he started a creamery. It was Clayton's work in Gooding, in particular in the establishment of cooperative creameries, that had a formative influence on his young son. In Idaho, indeed across much of the Western United States, dairy farmers were at the mercy of large food-processing companies. Swift and Company bought virtually all the dairy output in Idaho. As such, Swift could dictate to the farmers the price paid for milk and cream. Gradually, dairy farmers banded together, forming cooperatives to stand up to the giant companies like Swift. In the West, Challenge Cream and Butter represented those farmers who

The combination of his grandmother's voice and the vivid illustrations of Sir John Tenniel provoked the young Doug Strain to follow the rabbit and Alice down the hole, imagining himself so small that he was only the size of an electron.

shipped their produce to Los Angeles; Land'O Lakes fulfilled the same role for dairy farmers in the Mid-West.

As the young Douglas grew, he watched his father work within the dairy cooperative framework, absorbing the cooperative ethic that at its core represented an idealistic vision of teamwork, community values and the virtue of banding together to achieve something that no individual could accomplish on his own. This was a powerful lesson that would blossom years later in a young student and engineer.

At the same time, the other powerful influence in Doug's life remained his maternal grandmother, Cora Linn Crockatt. Herself an accomplished pianist and painter, Cora was saddened to see the boy show so little interest in art, and so little aptitude for music. Not willing to be defeated by the unfocused energies of a six year-old, she took to reading with her grandson. Soon, they embarked on Lewis Carroll's *Alice in Wonderland*, and the young boy was hooked. As he followed Alice down the rabbit hole, watching her grow and shrink, Doug became fascinated with the idea that Alice could grow small. But how small was small? He was aware that science had begun to ask the same question, Robert Millikan having received the Nobel Prize in Physics in 1923 for his measurement of the charge on an electron. "So I decided to imagine myself as small as an electron. What would that be like?" And as Doug wondered, he read more and more about electrons, more and more about physics. Years later, having started ESI, Strain used to administer a brief examination to applicants for engineering positions:

> Some of the people thought I was crazy because we had some questions on the exams for technicians coming in like: "If you were an electron and you came up to this binding post, what would you do?" And they would go "Arrgh!" Most of them did absolutely nothing with it and it was an off-the-wall question. But it's been a big help to me even today, because you're [finally] properly scaled. How do you know how big a gate can be in a chip if it's going to hold 10,000 electrons, for example, which is what most of them do? Now they're working toward one-electron gates with carbon nano tubes; they might even get there some day!

About the same time, by the end of the 1920s, the ten-year old Strain also made his first crystal radio set. Lying in bed at night, he picked up stations from San Francisco, or Salt Lake City and the Mormon Tabernacle Choir.

As if the tumblers in an exquisite lock were falling into place, Strain's interest in the tiny Alice, electrons and radio all coincided with the arrival of a twelve-volume engineering encyclopedia – a gift of his grandmother – in the Gooding Public Library. By the time he finished sixth grade, he had devoured all twelve. The lad with a fascination for electrons and radios had revealed the scholarly aspect of his character that would come to mark his entire career. But, at that moment, the family's life took an abrupt turn.

Throughout the 1920s American farmers lived on the edge of financial disaster. In the Mid-West the signs were more obvious than in the West. Closely tied to loans made to farmers, many banks began to fail. First farmers in the Mid-West, but as the Stock Market crashed in October, 1929, even the relatively prosperous farmers of the Pacific Northwest fell victim to the Depression. In Idaho farms failed, creameries closed, and the Challenge Cooperative made drastic changes. Of all their local managers, Clayton Strain stood out. He had gone back to Cornell for a Masters Degree in Dairy Manufacturing and now that decision paid off. Challenge brought him to their headquarters in Los Angeles, with the assignment to broaden the cooperative's line beyond milk and butter into ice cream, processed cheese, and dehydrated milk.

Clayton Strain arrived in Los Angeles in 1932, the family followed in 1933. "We came in with a big old trailer, and an old car full of stuff, and were stopped at the border. We had to demonstrate that we weren't 'Oakies.' Dad could show that he had a job, so they let us through. They held us up a few hours.. but we got in." For the young boy, California was eye-popping. "It was heaven. I mean Southern California in those days...." The family settled near Pasadena, and Doug enrolled at Alhambra High School, graduating in 1938. But it was overwhelming at first. Alhambra High seemed huge, with a student body three times the size of the entire town of Gooding. Nevertheless, he soon adjusted. "It was a good school. We had an excellent education, outstanding." Doug flourished. And not only were there classes, there were clubs: a science club, a math club, a scholarship club, a radio club. He was in them all, but his real love was radio.

And another tumbler falls into place. Grandmother Crockatt, who accompanied the family to California, lost little time in making it known that her precocious grandson was a radio whiz. "She dropped into the local radio service shop, called Elliott and Zimmerman Radio Laboratories, and said she had a grandson who was very expert with radio and would there be a job for him?" Sure enough, there was a job, sorting parts and making routine repairs. Now, as it happened, Messers Elliott and Zimmerman had both been engineers for Gilfillan Radio, Southern California's premier radio firm. With manufacturing licenses from RCA and Packard Bell, Gilfillan built all the radio sets contracted to Southern California distributors, such as Western Auto, Sears Roebuck and Montgomery Ward.

Elliott and Zimmerman, however, were first to install radios in cars, car radios designed and marketed by a young maverick, Paul Galvin. Galvin had decided that since RCA had developed the Victrola, and had called their first radios "Radiolas," if he was going to put one in a car, he would call his radio a "Motorola." "Paul Galvin showed up one day while I was buried underneath one of the cars... I remember sitting on a bench with him while he told us the story of how he named his company." Although he could not know it as he sat and listened to Galvin that afternoon, Doug Strain himself would be part of the birth of high technology. Indeed, the late Thirties was a wondrous era for the future development of the electronics industry! All over the country, in shops and garages, people such as Paul Galvin, Bill Hewlett and David Packard, Howard Vollum and Jack Murdock, met, tinkered, and began what would become the foundation of high technology in the United States: Motorola, Hewlett-Packard, Tektronix.

For Strain, installing and repairing radios was "really pretty easy." In those days most of the trouble happened with the filter capacitors in the radio's power supply. The capacitors would dry out, high voltage would break them down, and they would need replacement:

> You'd know they were dried out if the rectifier tube glowed blue. The set would come in. They'd have me turn it on. If the tube was blue, why they had a whole rack of these capacitors, and I'd just take them out, get the wrenches and bolt some new ones in and wire them up, and out it would go. That's all there was to it. So I was fixing about 90 percent of the sets with that simple repair. Just inspecting each to see if the tube glowed blue, which said it was drawing way too much current, because the gas was ionizing inside it; those filters were out and I'd go ahead and replace them.

Doug Strain (back row, second from right) editor in the fall of 1940 of the Pasadena Junior College Engineering Magazine.

So impressed were Mr. Elliott and Mr. Zimmerman, that they suggested the teenager apply for a better job at the Gilfillan plant, their former employer. So, during the summers of his sophomore and junior high school years, Strain had one of the most remarkable of Depression-era jobs: an indoor assembly job in high technology that paid between $7 and $8 a day.

Although Doug and his family certainly benefited from his summer work with Elliott and Zimmerman, his mother's commitment to community service turned the young high school student in a different direction during the summer of his senior year. For the next two summers Strain worked at the YMCA camp in the San Bernadino Mountains. Here, then, in the microcosm of his four high school summers, was the defining polarity in the future life of Doug Strain: electronics and community service. Without a doubt, by the time the young man departed for Pasadena Junior College in the fall of 1938, he was "hard wired" for these two poles. Indeed, he would spend his entire life devoted to making a lasting contribution in both the electronics industry and in the many communities he served.

Before World War II, for all practical purposes, electronics meant radio. This much was clear on a personal level from Strain's work with Elliott and Zimmerman; more broadly, to RCA, Philco, Zenith, Packard-Bell and others, electronics also meant radios for the American consumer. There was, however, a tiny segment of electronics attended by only a handful of scientists and engineers: instrumentation. A few companies, such as General Radio, Leeds and Northrop, and Dumont, made basic instruments for electrical measurement and calibration. In the Pasadena area, a small local company, Beckman Instruments, offered a modest line of basic chemistry test instruments. In his senior year in high school, Doug Strain called on Beckman (then called National Technical Laboratories) in conjunction with his senior science project:

It was to Melville Eastham's General Radio, GenRad, in Cambridge, Massachusetts, that other electronics companies looked to as a model for organization and business practices.

> A friend of my father had decided that brewer's yeast was just being wasted, taken away from breweries and dumped in landfills. [He thought] that you could make vitamin B complex out of refined brewer's yeast, but he needed to control the acidity on process. . . I had heard of Dr. Beckman's new glass electrode pH meters. . . So I went over to his little hole-in-the-wall plant and met with him and some of his people and said I had a high school project. I wanted to make a flow pH meter. So one of the guys was very good to me, gave me the electrometer tube, some of the special glass that had relatively low resistance so you could measure through it. . . . So I assembled this flow pH meter in my senior year in high school, and for that I got the Bausch and Lomb National Science Award . . .

Arthur O. Beckman was so pleased with the work of the senior award-winner that he offered Strain a part-time job at Beckman Instruments. In addition, he worked full time during his first two collegiate summers, and at the end of the war, when he was ready to resume his studies at Cal Tech, Strain once again worked at Beckman. Indeed, upon graduating from Cal Tech in 1948, his first job was at Beckman.

The War Years

In the space of four years, between 1942 and 1945, the United States remade itself. Gone were the bread lines, the crippling unemployment and the stagnant financial economy that had stifled economic growth. The signs of America's recovery were apparent by

1940, almost imperceptibly at first, as the nation began to prepare for war. The reintroduction of the Selective Service Act in September 1940 meant that Doug Strain, Merle Morgan, Lawrence Rockwood, and Charlie Davis, all future key employees of ESI, had to register for the draft. While a sample of four might be statistically insignificant, these are, nonetheless, the "Four Horsemen," and thus for ESI these four men are a critical sample. What is so remarkable is the fact that three of these four men spent the war in alternative service, having registered as conscientious objectors under the Selective Service Act. We have seen that Doug Strain came from a family deeply committed to community service bred from their missionary background in the Disciples of Christ. After he arrived in Pasadena, Doug gravitated toward the Quaker Church. Many of the same people who were involved in the co-operative movement in Southern California were active in the Friends, particularly the Orange Grove Meeting, one of the best-known Quaker meetings in the area. As he met new people in his Friends meetings and in the San Gabriel Valley Consumer Co-Op, Doug might unknowingly have crossed paths with another Southern California Quaker: Merle Morgan.

Merle Morgan was born in Whittier, California, in 1919. Almost exactly the same age as Doug Strain, Morgan came from a Quaker family. In fact, Whittier was a predominantly Quaker community, and when Merle's time came to register for the draft, like Doug Strain, he, too, filed 4E. A graduate of Whittier High School, Morgan had worked summers for the McCullough Tool Company, as a research engineer, designing electric well-logging instruments for use with the heavy oil-drilling equipment built by McCullough. He graduated from Fullerton Junior College and tested into Cal Tech in precisely the same way both Strain and Rockwood did. He entered Cal Tech in 1940, just a year before the other two.

Along with Merle Morgan, Lawrence Rockwood was a native Californian. He was born in Los Angeles in 1920. The family lived in Monrovia, east of Pasadena, and Rockwood graduated from Monrovia High School. Living with the family was Rockwood's uncle, Ray, his mother's brother. Uncle Ray was a science buff, very bright, and very eager to pass on his love of science to his young nephew. "He read to me from *Scientific American* and *Popular Mechanics* and those kind of things. He took me down in his shop in the basement and gave me the free run of working with the power tools and everything as a little kid." Ray was quite interested in electric power, power plants and power engineering and "aimed me in that direction." After high school Rockwood went on to Pasadena Junior College, taking advantage of the superb, free education. As did Doug Strain, Rockwood tested into Cal Tech for the fall of his junior year, 1941. In fact, Pasadena Junior College annually gave an Engineering Honor Key to the top engineering graduate. In 1941, PJC gave two keys: one to Rockwood, and one to Strain. Rockwood, too, had formative experiences in his part-time and summer jobs. During his collegiate summers, Rockwood worked at Lockheed, first doing quality control work, running tests at the end of a heat-treat oven on swing shift, then later in the engineering department. When Rockwood registered for the draft, unlike Strain and Morgan, he had received a straight student deferment. Thus able to complete his degree at Cal Tech, he graduated in 1943. "We were recruited [by private industry] like crazy at Cal Tech," Rockwood recalled. Most of the companies were on the East Coast, and all of them were large companies. Rockwood looked for something local and something small. "I hunted up a little outfit in South Pasadena, W.C. Robinette Company. Founded by a Cal Tech

Together with Lawrence Rockwood (fourth row, fourth from left), Doug Strain (fourth row, far right) was a member of the Pasadena Junior College Electrical Engineering Club.

Throughout the Thirties, the campus endured one construction project after another, until by 1941 the Cal Tech campus had grown from its relatively modest beginnings into a bustling center for advanced scientific training and research. It was here, in the fall of 1941 that Doug Strain, Merle Morgan and Rocky Rockwood crossed paths.

graduate, Willard C. Robinette, Robinette Company had a government contract from the Department of the Navy to develop a servo mechanism (the high-speed, electric, motor-driven system) for laying five-inch guns on destroyers. "Working for Robinette was a turbulent experience, because Mr. Robinette was himself a kooky character with quite a temper." Within a short time, however, Rockwood's draft board notified him that his number was coming up. Rather than push for a defense-related deferment, Rockwood followed his intuition, applying for a commission in the Navy.

After Navy boot camp at the Great Lakes Naval Training Station, Rockwood progressed to officer training at Fort Schuyler on Long Island, New York. His Cal Tech degree, his work with Robinette, and the Navy's own tests all pointed Rockwood in the direction of electronics, and ultimately radar. After extensive training in both radar and sonar at Bowdoin College, MIT and Harvard, Rockwood ended up in the Boston Navy Yard, checking radar on destroyers coming off the ways in Bath, Maine. At the end of the war he drew battleship duty, ferrying returning GIs back from Europe. Mustered out in 1946, Rockwood returned to Robinette Company in Los Angeles, where the company was hard at work trying to convert their gun-laying servo mechanisms to civilian commercial applications.

Lawrence Rockwood's war experience was similar to that of millions of other men who participated in key support roles rather than combat, roles that enabled the American forces to prosecute a vigorous and successful war. Indeed, in his case, the military made good use of his technical expertise, even enhancing it with further training. For a handful of others, though, the war years passed in very different fashion. Fewer than one-half of one percent of all men eligible for the draft registered as conscientious objectors, and only a fraction of those who did register 4E were actually granted that status by their draft boards. Three of those who were accorded conscientious objector (CO) status were Doug Strain, Merle Morgan and Charlie Davis.

Charlie Davis, the "Fourth Horseman," was born in 1919 in Oklahoma City. Davis attended elementary and high school in Oklahoma City and upon graduation from high school in 1937, the young Davis struck out for California and the University of Southern California. At USC he majored in accounting, graduating in 1941. Drafted in December 1941 as a CO, Davis found himself shipped to a former Civilian Conservation Corps (CCC) camp in Wyeth, Oregon, in the Columbia River Gorge near Cascade Locks. It was in Wyeth, in mid-January 1942, that Charlie Davis met Doug Strain. Strain and Merle Morgan, graced by Linus Pauling's intercession on their behalf, had completed the fall semester at Cal Tech, and then as COs were both immediately inducted into civilian alternative service by the U.S. military authorities. Morgan was shipped just down Route 66 about fifteen miles east of Pasadena to the San Dimas Forest Service Station, where the Quakers volunteered to coordinate a camp for COs. Here Morgan spent the war designing instrumentation and compiling and analyzing experimental data in the development of an electronic means to measure soil moisture at the electronics laboratory that the Forest Service maintained at the San Dimas Station. Strain, on the other hand, landed in the Wyeth CCC camp on January 15, 1942.

Both Davis and Strain recall that the Wyeth camp was in a decrepit state when they arrived. During the Depression the CCC built and maintained numerous camps throughout the United States. With the approach of war and the decline of the CCC, camps fell into disrepair. The Wyeth camp had housed CCC workers who maintained hiking trails, built and manned fire lookout towers, and fought forest fires. So, under the coordinating eye of the Mennonites and the Brethren, the COs set about to restore the camp, and pick up where the CCC had left off. For roughly a year Davis and Strain worked out of the Wyeth camp, in the summer ranging far and wide fighting forest fires, and the rest of the time doing maintenance work on Forest Service projects in the Columbia Gorge. Gradually, however, back in Washington, D.C. it dawned on Franklin Roosevelt's wartime Director of the U.S. Office of Scientific Research and Development (OSRD), Dr. Vannevar Bush, that perhaps technically-trained COs could be put to more creative uses than simply clearing trails and fighting forest fires.

Despite the occasional outburst from General William Hershey that COs were not being worked hard enough, Dr. Bush saw a different use for some of these young men. For almost a year, from August 1942 to May 1943, Charlie Davis was posted to the state mental hospital in Fort Steilacoom, Washington. After a short time back in the Columbia Gorge at Cascade Locks, Davis was shipped to Washington, D.C. to participate in the International Relief Training Agency, an experimental effort to put COs overseas doing relief work. He then worked in various capacities for the American Friends Service Committee for the remainder of the war.

Of the three COs, Doug Strain seems to have had the most varied wartime experience. The work in the Columbia Gorge was hard, but Doug was surprised at how much he enjoyed it. The Forest Service personnel took some time adjusting to a group of young men who were considerably more mature than had been the raw CCC conscripts. But adjust they did. ". . . We couldn't have been put with a better agency," recalled Strain, "because they really are mostly conservancy people at heart, and we fit in with their views on that, and we had some very good supervisors." Eventually, Strain was part of a group of COs from around the U.S. who were assembled at Walhalla, Michigan, for an unusual project. Many COs had experience in the cooperative movement, and Strain's own experience with consumer cooperatives in southern California, as well as his father's long history in the Co-Op movement, qualified him for selection for the Walhalla project. On his way to Michigan, he took an important furlough home to Southern California to marry his high school sweetheart, Leila Cleo Kanicofe. Doug and Leila had met as lab partners in freshman science class at Alhambra High School, and Leila by now had graduated from UCLA in bacteriology and was a licensed medical technician.

In a surprisingly tolerant move, the wartime government supported at Walhalla what amounted to a think-tank in Michigan to brainstorm new modes of social and industrial organization. During the day, the COs would plant trees, and in the evenings they would gather for the "Co-Op school." Many of the participants were deeply impressed with Sweden's system, then called "The Middle Way," that seemed to combine capitalism and socialism in a society less prone to the conflicts that had beset capitalist societies of the previous generation. Visiting speakers came, including socialist Norman Thomas; "We had some really good courses and good people," recalled Strain. In another project at Walhalla, a number of CO's, including Strain, volunteered as "guinea pigs" for a flu virus experiment sponsored by Bush's OSRD, in which everyone came down with one or more strains of influenza.

Former CCC Camp, Wyeth, Oregon, OrHi 015051

Crew from Wyeth, Oregon, OrHi 015050

In January 1942, Doug Strain and Charlie Davis met at the Wyeth Civilian Public Service Camp, a converted Civilian Conservation Corps camp. Operated by the Brethren and the Mennonites, the Wyeth camp dispatched its charges, conscientious objectors, into the woods along the Columbia Gorge, to clear trails, fight fires and fell trees, the wood from which would often be split by crews such as the one show here.

Doug Strain (second from right) and other "guinea pigs" in the cold room at the University of Illinois, in 1944.

After almost a year in Michigan, the Walhalla participants scattered to other assignments. Realizing that because of the draft many critical scientific projects were delayed or dormant for lack of technical manpower, Vannevar Bush, decided systematically to tap the manpower of the CO camps. Strain was assigned to the University of Illinois in yet another "guinea pig" study. The University of Illinois Medical School was conducting nutrition experiments to determine the effects of extreme cold on human caloric intake:

> The cold room was primarily to get our metabolism up so we'd burn lots of calories in a day, like 8000, or so. If you shiver all the time, you get thin in a hurry, and so they had us in these rooms at 20 below zero, and we shivered.... They were trying to figure out whether high-fat, high- carbohydrate or high-protein diets were best. . . . Mid-year we shifted to vitamins, looking at vitamin effects. We did controlled experiments all day, psychometric experiments, psychological experiments, visual experiments.

> . . . Dr. Warren McCullough, already a well-known neurologist was designing some of the experiments and used me as his technician in my spare time.. He was the guy I worked with. We worked nights and weekends, and did a lot of things together. He hadn't heard of feedback, electrical feedback; he was just looking at signals going out from the brain to control muscle response. Feedback was a new concept to him, so we began measuring human feedback. At Cal Tech we had learned to use feedback to control servo mechanisms, a form of automatic motion control of machines. He began writing papers on the human being as a servo mechanism. Warren was brilliant man and it was a real privilege to work with him. He eventually went on to MIT to work with mathematician Norbert Weiner, and the two founded the science of "cybernetics."

When this "guinea pig" project was over in late 1944, Strain was sent back to Oregon, this time out of the woods and into the Forest Service Radio Laboratory.

RADIO AND THE BIRTH OF TECHNOLOGY IN THE NORTHWEST 1945-1949

The "Brown Bridge" that Frank Brown built, with Doug Strain's help, for General Radio during World War II. After the war, Brown Engineering continued to manufacture the bridge, whose distinctive brown case, more than the company's name, gave it its name.

Radio In Portland

As the train carrying Doug Strain made its way from Chicago to Portland in the fall of 1944, everywhere he looked he could see the changes wrought by the war. And nowhere were the changes more evident than in the Northwest. As the train wound its way down the Columbia Gorge, the new aluminum plants in The Dalles and Troutdale confirmed the nation's voracious appetite for aircraft-related materials. Portland bristled with activity, its population swollen by the influx of war workers. The Kaiser Shipyards on Swan Island and in Vancouver and the Willamette Steel Shipyards in North Portland combined to produce more than a dozen Liberty Ships a month. A brand new city, Vanport, sprang up on the lowlands of Jantzen Beach to accommodate both black and white workers and their families. Amid the hum of new wartime heavy industry, a small electronics operation in southeast Portland, run by two brothers, Frank and Jesse Brown, made electronic instruments for the Army.

In retrospect, the birth of high technology in the Northwest appears easy to trace. At the time, however, its antecedents were far less obvious. Nowhere in the United States had Americans been immune from the Great Depression. In the Pacific Northwest, however, the Depression took on a somewhat different character. Heavily dependent on agriculture, logging and fishing, the essentially rural Northwesterners fell back on their pioneer roots to survive the privations that hit working-class men and women far harder in the industrial Midwest and East. Northwest financiers were loath to foreclose on farmers and loggers, preferring to defer payments rather than taking over farms and mills. Seattle, linked almost exclusively with timber and fishing, suffered more than Portland. Portland's economy, more diversified that her sister city to the north, rested on transportation, finance, and commerce. By the Thirties Portland's industrial base was well-established: the Electric Steel Foundry (later ESCO), the Willamette Iron and Steel Company (later WISCO), the Willamette Ersted Company (later Hyster), Portland Woolen Mills, Oregon City Woolen Mills, Pendleton Woolen Mills, Jantzen, and the Iron Fireman Manufacturing Company.

Even during the Depression, the diversified economy of Portland provided many of her citizens with a comfortable, middle-class standard of living compared to those living elsewhere. Indeed, in 1935, Portland ranked second, behind Long Beach, California, in "spendable family income," with an average of $3,382 per household. Not surprisingly, those who could afford it indulged in the purchase of the nation's newest entertainment technology: a radio. Indeed, from 1937 on, those who could afford a radio might well have gone to the shop of a young businessman, Jack Murdock, whose store was on Portland's east side, at 57th and Foster Rd. Here, in "the House that Jack Built," a young Jack Murdock sold appliances and radios: GEs, Philcos, RCAs and Stromberg-Carlsons. And, if your radio needed fixing, in the back of Murdock's shop a young man, Howard Vollum, operated a repair shop. Thus, at the same time the young Doug Strain was installing and repairing radios at Elliott and Zimmerman in Alhambra, the founders of Tektronix, Murdock and Vollum, were also engaged in radio sales and repair in Portland.

As previously noted, for those interested in electronics, radio was where the action was. Invented by Guglielmo Marconi in 1895, radio began to come into its own in 1904, when Sir John Fleming invented the vacuum electron tube that amplified Marconi's radio waves. With Fleming's vacuum tube, radio could now transmit the human voice, even music. Two years later, Lee de Forest invented the "audion," a type of triode that not only received radio waves, but amplified them as well. The First World War, and the military's need for long-range communication, gave radio an additional boost. General Electric, American Telephone and Telegraph and Westinghouse all began to produce radio equipment for the government. In 1919, the Radio Corporation of America (RCA) was formed. Although Westinghouse Company opened the first commercial radio station in 1920 in Pittsburgh, RCA was not far behind. By 1921, RCA was not only producing radio equipment, but as of 1926 had formed its own broadcasting network, the National Broadcasting Corporation (NBC).

What RCA understood was the immense potential of radio among American consumers. Virtually anyone with several dollars and a little spare time could buy the parts to make a crystal set. For slightly more, $22.50 to be exact, the consumer could buy RCA's basic radio receiver. And buy them the public did. In the 1920's radio became the ubiquitous item in every household with electricity, a medium linking a nation that, while unified, remained distinctly regional in its politics and culture. By the Thirties, radio had become the principle political instrument of President Franklin D. Roosevelt,

Harold Lawson, pioneer radio engineer of the Pacific Northwest, head of the Forest Service Region 6 Radio Lab, and later Chief Engineer for Doug Strain at Electro-Measurements and ESI.

whose steady and consoling voice reached every home and hearth during the Depression with his "fireside chats." Radio listeners in Portland could choose from over a dozen radio stations by the end of the Thirties. Among the earliest stations in town were KEX, KGW, KWJJ and KOIN. But consumer radio was not the only form of radio development in the Pacific Northwest.

The Forest Service Radio Laboratory

Since the turn of the century the United States Forest Service (USFS) had maintained an active interest in wireless communication. Even before World War I the USFS attempted to link its vast network of ranger stations, camps and fire lookout towers by means of telegraph lines. Advances in wireless radio communications during the war found a ready application in the USFS after the war. Although the USFS established a radio laboratory in Beltsville, Maryland, regional labs sprang up in each of the Forest Service's districts. In the Pacific Northwest, Region 6, the Forest Service Radio Lab was first located in Tacoma, Washington. It soon moved to Vancouver, Washington, and there, under the direction of Harold Lawson, the Forest Service Lab designed the rugged, portable, battery-operated radios the USFS needed in the field. The production of the USFS radios was contracted to Radio Specialty in Portland and Spokane Radio in Spokane. But quarters in Vancouver were cramped, and by 1931 Lawson and his crew were looking for a new location. As it happened, KEX had just finished building a new studio, vacating their old facilities out on the eastside of Portland on 122nd St.:

> Here were these two great, big radio towers, and the transmitter building, which was pretty good sized [recalled Strain], but the Forest Service took it over mostly, I think, because the brass back in Washington could understand these two big towers. . . But we never used them for a thing, never even raised a flag on them. We had to tear them down, eventually, because they were a hazard for the little airfield out there. But it was a stroke of genius [on Harold Lawson's part]. . . You know, it looked like a Navy installation, or something.

Harold Lawson is the grandfather of high technology in the Pacific Northwest. Born in 1904 and raised in Vancouver, Washington — no doubt a factor in his relocation of the Forest Service Radio Lab from Tacoma to Vancouver — Lawson was a self-taught radio expert. Although he briefly attended Oregon Agricultural College, he never finished college. He worked in the woods, started a radio station at Oregon Agricultural College, and eventually joined the Forest Service. His knowledge of radio soon brought him to the Region 6 USFS Radio Lab. As its director, by the mid-Thirties he led a small team of engineers, among them Logan Belleville, who with Vollum and Murdock of Tektronix, would become one of Tek's founding engineers. As war came, the compass of Lawson's contacts would widen, bringing him in touch with other pioneers of electronics in the Northwest, in particular Frank Brown and Doug Strain.

With the outbreak of the Second World War, Lawson's work at the Forest Service Developmental Lab took on new urgency. In a letter after the war Doug Strain described the Lab's wartime challenge:

> During the war, [Harold Lawson's] job was complicated by the Air Raid Warning Service, which became a responsibility of the Forest Service. Suitable communications equipment was not available for Air Raid Warning purposes

and even after the Laboratory had developed prototype equipment, there was no place for such a civilian agency to let contracts. Mr. Lawson took the bull by the horns, turned the laboratory facilities into a manufacturing plant, hired a work force, and with only civilian priorities, began the manufacture of the necessary equipment. That this program was successfully carried out under such circumstances indicated the resourcefulness of the man and his substantial managerial ability.

The Realities of the Wet Woods

Thus it was that the unlikely spot of Portland, Oregon, whose infrastructure and infant industries had nothing to do with electronics, developed into one of the nation's leading centers for the development of practical, rugged, portable field radio equipment. And it was to a grateful Harold Lawson, short of manpower, that the young Doug Strain reported in the late fall of 1944. Strain quickly learned that even under wartime pressure, when red-tape was at a minimum, balancing the realities of the field with the demands of Washington was often an exercise in frustration. Lawson needed a relatively low transmission frequency for the new equipment the lab was to produce, since the dense, wet forest foliage absorbed and reflected microwave frequencies and blocked the signal. The Pentagon refused his requests, insisting he use the high frequency band they had assigned for the project. The result was that equipment did not perform well in the field, and Lawson was forced to travel to Washington to plead his case:

> [The high frequency equipment] wouldn't work in the forest, because the wet forest just absorbed that frequency. You'd go twenty feet into the forest and you were dead. It was amusing, because I remember Harold coming back and telling us about his visits [to Washington]. Some guys would come in with this high frequency stuff, which could be made much more compact than [the equipment] we were making, demonstrate it and they could show [that it worked]. He said, "well, it won't go around corners, etc, etc. . . ." Well, they did it in the halls of the Pentagon. The walls were so reflective they could get around the corners, and they convinced themselves that we were liars out here. . . . So Harold went back [to Washington] again. He was very mild-mannered, very clever and very smart. And he said, "Well, that's very interesting, I guess, and I can see why you would believe it, but please, will you send two of your best men out with this equipment to me, and let's try it out in the forest?" And so these men came out, you know, the big brass. They walked about thirty feet into the forest in the Columbia Gorge, right up one of those trails . . . . absolutely dead signal, just quit . . . . Nothing like a field test!

Having proved his point, Lawson got his low frequency band assigned and could now fulfill the government contract with equipment that met specifications and that functioned in the real world.

Moonlighting on the Bridge

Doug Strain worked with Harold Lawson at the Forest Service Developmental Lab, at the crossroads of electronics in Portland, indeed the Northwest. Even before the war Lawson and his crew had played a central role in the proceedings of the Portland chapter of the Institute of Radio Engineers, where radio enthusiasts met on a monthly basis to exchange information and to discuss the latest techniques. Thus, when a radio or electronics engineer needed help with a problem, any problem, he would turn to Lawson

Portland, Oregon, aerial photo, 1944, OrHi 69911

When Doug Strain arrived in Portland in the fall of 1944, he found a city transformed for war production. Seen here from the Ross Island Bridge looking north, shipbuilding along the Willamette included naval escort vessels, destroyers and even an aircraft carrier. Farther north, along the banks of the Willamette and on the Vancouver shores of the Columbia River, the Kaiser Shipyards, Willamette Steel and Oregon Shipyards all built Liberty Ships.

and his lab. And in early 1945 just such a man with a problem came to the lab in hopes of some help. That man was Frank Brown, and his problem was the same as virtually every other wartime defense contractor: labor.

Frank Brown was a native of Klamath Falls, Oregon. A man with considerable mechanical and technical skill, Brown had opened a radio repair shop in Klamath Falls. Since virtually everyone who had a radio in Klamath Falls at one time or another needed a new tube or service on a radio, Frank came into contact with most folks in town. One of those folks, Melville Eastham, ultimately left Klamath Falls. Under Eastham's leadership, he and Arthur Thiessen went on in 1915 to found what had become one of the nation's leading electronics instrument companies: the General Radio Company (GenRad) in Cambridge, Massachusetts. When war broke out in 1941, government officials, fearing that the concentration of America's most sensitive defense industries on the Eastern Seaboard made the country too vulnerable to aerial attack from the Atlantic, ordered many companies to disperse their operations. Washington told GenRad to get out of the Boston area, and as a result, Eastham, recalling earlier days in Klamath Falls, decided to locate a small part of their operation there. Eastham remembered the young man in the radio repair shop, Frank Brown, and asked him to head up the assembly of a large government contract for GenRad's impedance bridges, an instrument also known as an RCL meter, that measures the values of resistors, capacitors and inductors, which are the major building-blocks of electronics. GenRad would ship him the parts, and Brown would assemble them in Klamath Falls.

While Klamath Falls had plenty of farmers, loggers and railroad workers, there were few hands available to assemble impedance bridges as they arrived in kits from the East. It did not take Frank Brown, and by now his brother Jesse, long to move their operation to Portland, where they hoped they could find a more readily available supply of labor, and where, when they needed to, they could scrounge the occasional spare parts necessary to complete each bridge. So it was natural, then, for Frank Brown to turn to Harold Lawson at the Forest Service Developmental Lab for spare parts, and, most importantly, spare labor.

Brown immediately recruited Strain and several others to moonlight after hours and on weekends to help in the assembly of impedance bridges. When he needed more parts, Frank would hustle off to the Forest Service Lab. This practice was still evident in the late Forties and early Fifties, when both Tektronix and Brown Engineering were on Hawthorne Blvd. in Portland and either Howard Vollum or Doug Strain would wander up to the other's shop to chew the fat and scrounge some spare parts. But when the parts were not available, as in the case of the bakelite moldings to be supplied by GenRad for the circuits of the bridge, Brown hired a couple of men to make molds of the parts. The War Production Board found an injection molding machine for Brown, and from these early molding efforts sprang the plastics company known as Grant and Roth Plastics that still operates in Portland today.

General Radio's contract kept Frank Brown's operation going for the duration of the war and on into the postwar years. Even as they worked to produce the 400 impedance bridges the GenRad contract called for, Brown and Strain made subtle improvements in the instrument. One of the elements of production was a 1,000 cycle tone generator. It was complex, die-cast and very expensive. They were scarce, and they were too expensive to make in Portland. Strain and Brown came up with a solution:

Klamath Falls Street Scene, 1944, OrHi 72049

In 1944, the boyhood home of GenRad's Melville Eastham, Klamath Falls, had the look of a prosperous rural town. Dominated by lumber and agriculture, and home to an Army Air Corps training field, Klamath Falls was also Frank Brown's hometown. But when Eastham offered Brown a contract to make resistance bridges for GenRad, Brown could not find the labor he needed, necessitating his move to Portland.

So we made a little hummer, a little vibrating reed that stood up on the part that we could machine out of strip stock. We guarded [i.e., shielded] it so it couldn't provide leakage down the side, which General Radio had never done. . . [We tuned] the vibrating reed to 1,000 cycles. So you'd hear it in headphones. . . and made a major improvement, because GR had neglected the capacitance across the bridge arms that our shielding eliminated.

So the Brown bridge worked better than the GenRad bridge. "We thought we could market it after the war, because it was more accurate than GR's. One of the distributors in New York, Colonel Burlingame of Burlingame and Associates, came out and thought he could market it." For Brown and Strain, postwar possibilities beckoned.

With the end of the war, however, came the end of most defense contracts, demobilization and the end of alternative service. Ten million GIs came home, to families, to jobs, to college. Lawrence Rockwood served out his tour in the Navy, returning to Los Angeles and the Robinette Company. Charlie Davis stayed on to work with the American Friends Service Committee. Both Merle Morgan and Doug Strain returned to Cal Tech in 1946. Much had happened in physics and electrical engineering during the past four years, not the least of which was the Manhattan Project and the creation of the atomic bomb. Where in 1939 there had been fewer than 100 physicists in the U.S., now there were thousands. The work that Morgan and Strain had done in 1941 was obsolete, and they had to begin their studies again. In 1948 both men graduated from Cal Tech in electrical engineering, Morgan determined to press on to graduate school, Strain eager to find work.

BROWN ELECTRO-MEASUREMENT 1949–1953

Brown Electro-Measurements, 4635 SE Hawthorne Boulevard.

The Post War Economy

The Second World War altered the landscape the world over. Where in Europe and Japan the destructive power of the war left tens of millions homeless, cities and entire regions reduced to rubble, in the United States the war years produced an economic boom the likes of which had never been seen. Under the necessities of U.S. wartime mobilization, the massive social and economic change surprised even the planners themselves. While the Depression seemed only a bad memory, now those same strategists confronted the demographic, social and economic changes wrought by the war years. Mobilization had opened opportunities to women and blacks, and during the first postwar generation American society gradually, grudgingly, began to concede to both women and blacks the rights commensurate with their wartime contributions.

The rise in wages during the war, combined with enforced saving and rationing, created pent-up consumer demand that could only be slaked by the return of a broad, consumer-based economy after the war. Having fought in the jungles of the Pacific, the sands of North Africa, the mountains of Italy and the bitter cold of Europe's winter of 1944-1945, the GIs came home to claim the fruits of their victory. For a time, the American economy struggled to convert from defense to peacetime production. But by 1948, assembly lines turned once more to cars and Kelvinators. And where would the new cars and refrigerators go? Into the new houses that sprang up in what was the nation's greatest housing boom.

Perhaps no sector of the American economy was as profoundly effected by the war and by the free spending of the postwar years than the electronics industry. While William Levitt planted houses on Long Island and set the pace for postwar suburban development, and while Ford, GM, and Chrysler put cars in the garages and carports of Levitt's houses, the telltale antennae on the roofs of America's suburban bungalows heralded the coming of the television age. Within a generation, virtually every household in America would feel the effect of wartime developments in electronics.

Postwar Portland

The war produced a richer America, an America on the verge of socially progressive reform, an America increasingly united by the automobile and the world's greatest highway system. The migration of workers and their families that began during the war would continue, transforming entire regions. Nowhere was the change more profound than in the West. In the four years of war, California was transformed by the breathtaking growth of the aircraft, ship-building, and electronics industries. Washington's growth, attributable to Boeing, to the Bremerton Navy yards and to the Manhattan Project's Hanford Reservation, breathed fresh life into her established timber, agricultural and fishing industries.

While the scale of things in Oregon was hardly as dramatic as California, or even neighboring Washington, growth was nevertheless impressive. During the war Kaiser shipyards blossomed both in Vancouver, Washington, and in Portland on Swan Island. Combined with an influx of workers for the Oregon Shipbuilding Company's St. Johns yard, as well as for some 700 other war-related industries, these wartime workers produced a dramatic demographic change in greater Portland. At its peak, Kaiser employed almost 100,000 people in its yards. The productive capacity of Kaiser's shipyards is legendary; during the peak period from late 1944 to early 1945, a new Liberty Ship left the ways in Vancouver every other day.

To meet the demands of her vastly increased workforce, Portland resorted to a variety of solutions, from radically redesigned bus service, to the creation of a brand new community: Vanport. At war's end, then, the Pacific Northwest teemed with demobilized soldiers and war workers eager to return to a peacetime economy. Among both demobilized soldiers and civilian war workers were thousands of scientists, engineers and electrical technicians. Many wanted to return to homes elsewhere in the U.S., but many had come to love the Pacific Northwest and intended to stay. In 1944 Henry Kaiser had surveyed his 91,000 workers in the Portland area and established that 52 percent of them wanted to remain in the Portland area. The survey revealed that worker satisfaction with the Portland metropolitan area was extremely high.

Wartime production in the Portland area was almost entirely heavy industrial, shipbuilding and metals fabrication. Boeing had a plant in Portland, and the textile mills of Portland supplied numerous defense contracts. But the electronics industry was located elsewhere. Before the war the single significant electronics company in Portland was Radio Specialties, doing contract work for the Forest Service. "Radio Spec," as it was

The "Brown Bridge" prominently displayed at the Norman B. Neely Enterprises booth at a trade show in the late 1940's.

known, worked closely with Harold Lawson's laboratory. Indeed, Frank Brown often turned to Radio Spec for help and support building his impedance bridges.

Victory in 1945 created a windfall for infant electronics companies. With the end of the war in August 1945, the American government had on its hands literally billions of dollars worth of highly sophisticated parts and equipment for which there was suddenly little or no demand. The government sold such surplus, often for only several pennies on the dollar. Electronics companies all over America reaped the benefits of such surplus sales. Particularly grateful for the windfall were start-up companies, struggling to get their first products to market. Brown Electronics and Tektronix, Oregon's two original high technology companies, capitalized of the opportunity to snap up surplus parts, making Portland the center for Oregon's future high technology industry.

Brown Electro-Measurement

Throughout the two years from 1946 to 1948, as he was completing his degree at Cal Tech, Doug Strain kept several irons in the fire. He resumed working part-time during the school year and full-time during summers with Beckman Instruments in South Pasadena, and when he graduated from Cal Tech in 1948, more out of loyalty than deep conviction, Strain went to work full-time for Beckman. While at Beckman Instruments, Doug worked on a number of projects, including a small portable pH meter, and the review and classification of electrometer tube characteristics for quality control in the production department. The most important work, however, was on a new spectrophotometer, an instrument to analyze the light spectrum given off by an incandescent source. He helped design a new optical mount that made it possible to employ a Féry prism for the first time in a practical instrument, by rotating the prism in front of a narrow slit in the instrument so that a photo tube could measure a very narrow band of light, indicating how much energy was absorbed in each frequency of the light spectrum. In addition to this breakthrough, he helped to develop a new amplifier and power supply for the spectrophotometer, working closely with Raytheon Company to produce a subminiature electrometer tube. Doug's work on the instrument's voltage regulator circuit ultimately led to the development of the Model B Spectrophotometer, which operated from standard household AC power and was one of Beckman's most successful instruments of its day.

Doug Strain, having just returned to Portland in 1948.

But every chance he got, Doug came north for a visit. Indeed, he made a trip north to Portland immediately after graduation in the spring of 1948, right in the middle of the famous Vanport flood. Meeting with Frank, Doug learned that Brown was just about out of orders, his wartime contracts having run their course. It was clear from their conversation that Doug probably would not long remain at Beckman. Talking further, Doug realized that Frank was scared; there were no real orders on the horizon. As he and Doug talked, they began to dream about a portable impedance bridge, one that combined size and portability with new features. Strain had done some design work at Beckman that led to the "Helipot;" why not use a similar design for a decade potentiometer in a new bridge? So they sketched out a design, integrating in it the new decade potentiometer, or "Dekapot." "Frank was a really good mechanical design engineer," recalled Strain, so "we had a nice little portable box, and didn't have any expensive parts in it." They used silver switches from an outfit in Chicago, OAK Manufacturing, that manufactured high frequency radio parts, high-quality inexpensive silver contacts, and "we really came up with a much better instrument and could sell it for three-hundred bucks."

While Frank Brown worked on the details of their design, Doug returned to Pasadena and Beckman Instruments. But by the spring of 1949 he resigned from Beckman and headed back north for good. Frank Brown had originally founded his company, Brown Engineering Company, in July of 1944, with a cash outlay of $1500. In February 1946, Jesse Brown joined his brother, putting up $1475 for a quarter interest in the company.

Doug Strain arrived March, 1949. The earliest minutes of their new company reveal that Frank sold another quarter interest to Doug for $1000 in cash and equipment, "and other assets valued at $315," and on May 9, 1949, the date of the first meeting of the Board of Directors, Brown Engineering Company became Brown Electro-Measurement, Corporation (BECO). There were three shareholders: Frank Brown had a 50% ownership, with 30 Class A Shares and 70 Preferred Shares; Doug Strain had a 25% stake, with 30 Class A Shares and 20 Preferred Shares; and Frank's brother Jesse Brown also had a 25% stake, with 30 Class A Shares and 20 Preferred Shares. All three, Frank, Doug and Jesse were Directors. On the Board, Frank Brown held the title of Chairman, Doug Strain that of Secretary. As corporate officers, Frank was President, Doug was Vice-President, and Jesse was Secretary/Treasurer.

Brown Electro-Measurement was, by any standard, a small company. In addition to the two Brown brothers and Doug Strain, there was only a handful of other people working in the little building at 4635 SE Hawthorne Boulevard. One of the earliest employees, Armen Grossenbacher, came to work for BECO in 1951, and at that time there were only eight employees. Armen Grossenbacher was a local boy, born in 1928 in Oregon City. He graduated from high school in 1946 and joined the U.S. Navy. Based in the Bay Area, the young rating qualified for radio and electronics school. Graduating at the top of his class, Grossenbacher landed on the aircraft carrier *Boxer* as part of the electronics division aboard ship. Mustered out in 1948, Grossenbacher took advantage of the GI Bill. After a year of college, however, he realized that it was electronics that really held his interest. Enrolling in the DeVry Electronics Institute in Chicago, one of the nation's leading electronics trade schools, he headed east in 1949. Two years later, degree in hand and newly married, he headed back to Portland.

Taking advantage of the job postings at the institute, Grossenbacher pursued openings, first at Tektronix, and ultimately at Brown Electro-Measurement. "I remember going to Tektronix and interviewing. They had 250 people, and I thought, 'Well, this place is way too big.'" So Armen Grossenbacher knocked on BECO's door:

> Doug looked at my resume. He said, "You're just the kind of person we're looking for, I want you to come to work for me and help me build a business," and that was love at first sight.... I didn't know what I was getting into, but I knew I liked this man, and this man wanted me, and he was electronics, and it was a new adventure. So, you know, how could anything be wrong?

The next day, he found out just how small BECO really was. "We all did everything." There were several women (they were referred to as "girls" in those days), who did much of the assembly work, but in reality everyone did a bit of everything, from

The BECO "Dekapot" that Doug Strain and Frank Brown designed in 1948. The Dekapot became the heart of the new resistance bridge the two would produce in the coming months and would lead to an entire generation of components considered state-of-the-art in the electronics industry.

final assembly, to making mechanical parts. "I learned how to [operate a] lathe, how to set up a lathe, a sanding machine, drill presses, even punch presses." Then, when the part was finished, "you went over to the other side of the building and assembled the parts." One thing Grossenbacher noticed was that the rate of shipping was, if anything, sporadic. After all the parts-making and assembly, "Sometimes you went over and put it in a box and shipped it. That was great." But so irregular was the shipment of instruments that things were very tight. "The wages were bare minimum... and I remember Doug asking me, 'It would be helpful if you [despite all Grossenbacher's electronics training from the Navy and the DeVry Institute!] would enroll in the local apprenticeship program, so they will pay some of your wages.'" More than once, BECO could not make its payroll until a customer's check came in. Usually delayed by only a day or two, the payroll would get out, and people lived very close to the edge. But what was lost in the promptness of the payroll was more than made up for in the family atmosphere of the intimate little company, and the pride of building such high-precision instruments. That sense of intimacy and family, a feeling shared by ESI employees well into the Seventies, began in an era when, for instance, Cleo Strain, Doug's wife, would bring in a roaster at Christmas and cook a turkey. Gifts were exchanged among friends, and a sense of accomplishment united BECO workers and their families.

The personal sacrifices employees made in waiting for postponed pay checks told only part of the story. All companies need cash, regardless of size or how successful they are, and indeed the history of companies can in no small measure be told in the history of their banking. The history of Brown Electro-Measurement/Electro Scientific Industries is no different. From the outset the company needed money. Two weeks after incorporating, on May 23, 1949, the three shareholders met as the Board of Directors to open a bank account at the First National Bank of Portland. Six days later they decided to borrow from the bank. On May 26, 1949, Brown Electro-Measurement signed a note for a $1000 loan from First National. In July 1949 Brown Electro-Measurement borrowed $5000 from the Reconstruction Finance Corporation. By August, they needed another $2500, which they got from the First National Bank. By the spring of 1950, Frank, Doug and Jesse again hit up First National, for $4000 in February and $10,000 in June.

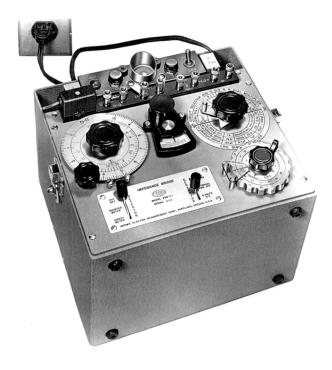

Why did the three need so much money in such quick succession? Quite simply, they were engineering the company's first portable impedance bridge, the Model 250. They knew they had a good instrument; it looked different than GenRad's impedance bridge, and it worked better. They were confident that it was also better than any bridge built by Leeds & Northrup, the other major instrument manufacturer. When East Coast distributors stopped in Portland on their western swing, they seemed interested. One of the most important of these distributors, Colonel Burlingame, head of Burlingame & Associates, thought he could market the Model 250. But the expansive Burlingame failed to produce. There was a West Coast alternative to Burlingame, however: Neely Enterprises. Founded by Norman B. Neely an exceptionally gifted marketeer, Neely Enterprises became the western distributor for a number of West Coast electronics firms, including Hewlett-Packard, Tektronix and Brown Engineering.

The marriage between distributor and company was a particularly crucial relationship. The company depended upon the distributor to market and service the instruments, while the distributor had a great stake in the quality of the product and the ability

The BECO Model 250 Impedance Bridge. The brown crackle paint finish, the Dekapot and clean layout of the instrument's face, and the standard power cord were all early marks of BECO's new bridge.

A pair of Model 250's occupy pride of place in BECO's booth at the WESCON show in Long Beach in 1952.

of the company to respond to changing market conditions. "None of us had a large enough product line to justify establishing a national sales organization [at that time]," recalled Dave Packard. "I think you could also say," added Bill Hewlett, "looking at other people and ourselves, we definitely were technically-oriented companies. We didn't necessarily have knowledge of how to sell, and this marketing group had a great deal of knowledge of how you would sell. So this complemented, you might say, what was a weakness in many of these organizations. . . ." Indeed, Doug Strain recalled visits by Neely, who came to Portland personally to inspect the engineering and production at Brown Electro-Measurement and Tektronix.

The distributorship concept was perfectly suited to the infant electronics industry. Unable to support either a sales or service network, young companies could associate with a distributor, who, for a commission, would market instruments and provide service and support after the sale. In both sales and service, Neely was a cut above his competitors. He pioneered the traveling lab, first one, and then an entire caravan of trucks and vans crammed full of the latest electronics gear that Neely would take on extended junkets throughout the western states to laboratories, military installations, and university campuses, to demonstrate the latest equipment. Often engineers from several of the companies Neely represented would accompany the caravan. Years later Bill Hewlett would recall the sales caravan: ". . . Neely had the idea that you get a big truck, an enclosed van, and put all the equipment in it, everybody's equipment, and he'd go someplace like Hughes [Aircraft Company]. Now, you could attract everybody, you see, and you get the whole technical staff of Hughes out to come and go through this thing. It was a very, very effective marketing means. . . ." Indeed, years later, ESI would dispatch its own caravans, first to demonstrate its analog computer, the ESIAC, and later its early laser systems.

Neely Enterprises seemed to work well for Hewlett-Packard and Tektronix. Initially, however, for Brown Electro-Measurement, the results were less impressive in marketing the Model 250 Impedance Bridge. The three founders knew the Model 250 was a superi-

Although no picture exists of the BECO booth at the IEEE show in 1950, it was far more modest than the company's booth at the IEEE shown here in 1953 in New York.

or instrument. If they could only get the right people to stop and see the Model 250, to witness its performance and to see for themselves how accurate it was. Years later, in 1960, in his application for Senior Membership in the Institute of Radio Engineers, Doug Strain explained what made the Model 250 so special:

> As "Director of Research and Development" (a bigger title than the job!) I developed the BECO Model 250 series of portable impedance bridges. The accuracy of these instruments was extended into the 0.1% class by the introduction of a new form of slidewire which permitted convenient four place readings in a compact coaxial structure. The excellent accuracy and frequency response of this slidewire made it usable for high accuracy bridges in the audio frequency range. This element was patented and trademarked as the "Dekastat." Out of this structure grew other trademarked and patented structures such as the "Dekapot" voltage divider and "Dekatran" ratio transformer. After ten years the ESI Model 250 bridge still stands as the only universal impedance bridge in its accuracy class.

By 1950, with their operation deeper and deeper in the red, the three men, Frank, Doug and Jesse, decided that Brown Electro-Measurement would have to take the plunge and show its instrument at the Institute of Electrical and Electronic Engineers (IEEE) show in New York City.

Bill Hewlett and the "Big Break"

In March of 1950 Doug Strain set off for New York City and the IEEE show, with a Model 250 and several other items. Taking a closet-sized room at the old Barbazon Plaza Hotel, Strain made his way to Madison Square Garden with his equipment to set up the BECO booth. "You could buy a cardboard booth that you'd put together, painted nicely with 'Brown Electro-Measurement.' We were in the back row, you know, with our ten-foot booth, breaking the bank, costing us $550 for the booth.' And there he stood, hoping to attract some attention. But it was, after all, the back of the hall, so traffic was slow:

I had this little bridge sitting there with a sign about all the things it could measure and how accurate it was, and so forth and so on. And Bill Hewlett, whom I didn't know at the time, came by. And he had his badge on so I recognized him as Bill Hewlett of Hewlett-Packard, which already was pretty widely known. He looked at the bridge, and he looked at the sign, and said, "So you can do all that, huh? You say you can measure milliohms with it?" And I said, "Yup, milliohms." "Well, here," said Bill, taking out his hotel key and marking a fraction of the key off with his fingers, "tell you what, I want you to measure it from there to there." And I got about 30 milliohms. He said, "Okay, now just half of that, from here to here." So I moved my little clips around, and got 15 milliohms. "Pretty dang good!" he said, and he put his key back into his pocket and went ambling on down the aisle without any further comment. I got back to my hotel that night, and my mailbox was stuffed full. He had gone around to all the reps, all his company reps, and said, "Pick these guys up!"

This was the break BECO had hoped for. Hewlett-Packard had a distributor network, with independent sales representatives throughout the country, and even overseas. Smaller companies, and especially start-up companies such as BECO, could not afford their own sales force, so they relied on sales representatives, Burlingame or Neely, to sell their products. At the mercy of independent representatives, many companies never could "break out." Thus, when Bill Hewlett liked what he saw, and told all of the "H-P" representatives at the show about BECO and its remarkable little bridge, it opened a whole new world to the struggling company.

Having set out for New York alone, Doug Strain returned, in effect, with a worldwide sales force. The network of independent Hewlett-Packard sales representatives would continue to promote the BECO/ESI instrument line until 1963, when H-P decided to create their own sales force. "They always gave us time at all their sales meetings to make our pitch. They did the same for John Fluke and for Tektronix. We all marketed in those early days through H-P reps." As long as BECO, Fluke and Tektronix were not in direct competition with H-P, the arrangement worked. In the case of Tektronix, competition emerged rather quickly, since both Tektronix and H-P made oscilloscopes. Having used Neely enterprises as their distributor, Tektronix decided in 1950 to create its own sales force.

Doug Strain recalled how, at electronics shows, everyone pitched in to help construct booths and set up equipment. In the late Forties and early Fifties the electronics industry was a small fraternity, close-knit and supportive. If there was an ethic shared throughout the early electronics industry it came from General Radio. In what can only be described as a spectacularly successful mixture of idealism and quasi-socialistic management practices, GenRad set the standard not only in the manufacture of electronics gear, but in how a successful electronics company should run. Thus, early competitors fashioned themselves in GenRad's image. "Eastham occasionally returned to Klamath Falls," recalled Strain, clearly still awed by the elder statesman of the electronics industry, "and we loved it that he made a point of stopping by to see us when he was in Portland." Bill Hewlett and Dave Packard, Howard Vollum and Jack Murdock, John Fluke, and Frank Brown and Doug Strain, all created egalitarian company environments with few artificial boundaries between workers and management. Perhaps there was, and remains to this day, something special about companies whose heart is engineering, particularly electrical engineering. For essentially, electrical engineering is highly creative work, calling upon imagination and a willingness to experiment, often with unconventional ideas and unlikely solutions. With such a premium on creativity, rigid or authoritarian management simply would not work.

Beginning with his arrival in 1949 at Brown Electro-Measurement, it was clear that Doug Strain was the company's most creative engineer. So absorbed were Frank and Doug during 1949 and early 1950 in perfecting the design and the circuitry of the Model 250, that whatever differences lay between the two were completely submerged in their work. For the remainder of 1950, the orders that Doug brought back from New York were enough to keep the little company on Hawthorne Blvd. humming. And there were other orders, too. Of all the business in 1950, perhaps the most interesting was the contract from the Signal Corps for impedance bridges, spare parts and instruction manuals.

With the onset of the Cold War in the late Forties and by 1950 with the ripening of hostilities in Korea that engaged a United Nations force consisting principally of U.S. soldiers, sailors and airmen, the American military became one of the electronics industry's most important customers. Some companies, Tektronix, for instance, eschewed government contracts, telling Washington that they could buy Tek scopes "off the rack" or go elsewhere, since government contracts came with too many strings attached and Washington was notoriously slow to pay its bills. By 1950, Tektronix was already successful enough, and the Tek oscilloscope was so good, that Vollum, Murdock and company could afford to turn government contracts away. But BECO was not as fortunate. Indeed, the Signal Corps contract, which was for only $11,148.94, was critical to the company in two ways.

First, and most practically, the Signal Corps contract provided collateral for the First National Bank's loan. Having borrowed a total of $14,000 from the bank that spring, BECO signed over "the income and proceeds" from the Signal Corps contract in August 1950. This was enough to please the bank, and to enable BECO to increase its line of credit in February 1951 to $15,000, and again in May of that year to $25,000.

Second, and far more importantly, the Signal Corps contract itself marked an important engineering moment for Brown Electro-Measurement. Soon after the end of the Second World War, as the American military moved from piston-driven aircraft to jet propulsion and rocketry, and from early radar to much more sophisticated global radar warning systems, the Pentagon realized the need for vastly improved electrical measurement standards. If U.S. Air Force and Signal Corps equipment was to perform properly, instruments had to be calibrated, adjusted and tuned to precise tolerances and frequencies. This was especially important where jet aircraft were concerned, since with every design improvement a jet's electronics became more complicated and more sensitive. Just as important, field testing of Signal Corps communications gear demanded that the test equipment itself be calibrated before technicians could venture with it into the field.

Since his high school days, Doug Strain had maintained a passion for measurement standards. Anticipating the coming importance of precision standards, he had quietly submitted the Model 250 to a variety of standards laboratories in hopes of meeting the specifications – the international standards orders (ISO's) – of the International Standards Organization, the certification of the highest precision. Thus, Doug Strain recalled, when the Signal Corps came calling in 1950, BECO had already established the quality controls in the manufacturing process at the Hawthorne plant that enabled the company to meet the government's specifications:

The Signal Corps gave us one of the first contracts because our bridge was ten times more accurate than the GR [General Radio] bridge. GR never came back and matched our accuracy, and in the end it came out that we actually became nearly one hundred times more accurate. The GR instrument eventually faded out, and they were going on to other things, and not too successfully. They got into the oscilloscope business, but didn't make it. By this time, GR was just a little too late, against Tektronix, against Hewlett-Packard, and against us.

Things Come Apart

With the beginning of the Korean War in 1949, many reservists, eventually Jesse Brown among them, were summoned once again to service. Jesse Brown was the company's business manager. A graduate of the Woodbury Business School in Los Angeles, Jesse kept the books, maintaining the day-to-day bookkeeping and business functions of BECO. He got along well with the handful of employees. "He had a much more approachable personality [than his brother Frank]," recalled Strain, "and got along well with the [assembly] girls...." But he did not get along all that well with his brother. Jesse "wanted to move out and do some other things; the place wasn't making any real money to support the people we had." Thus, in 1951 his recall to service came at an opportune moment for Jesse Brown.

Doug Strain's passion for precision and his equal passion for meeting the almost impossible criteria of standards labs would become the hallmark of Brown Electro-Measurement, and of its successors, Electro-Measurements, Inc, and Electro Scientific Industries. It was not that Frank Brown failed to share Doug's passion for precision, but by 1951 an element of tension had crept into the relationship of the two men and into the management of their company.

For several years prior to his exit from the company, Jesse, and to a lesser extent his brother Frank, had repatriated preferred shares back to the company. In an effort to infuse additional capital into the struggling BECO, Doug Strain had purchased shares in October of 1950, acquiring 35 shares for $5,500 in cash. This meant that Frank Brown held 70 preferred shares, Doug Strain 55, and Jesse none. While technically still the majority shareholder, Frank Brown seemed less and less comfortable in the company. The period 1951 to 1953 was an increasingly difficult one for Frank Brown. The slow increase in orders and the growing sophistication of the work at BECO were leaving Frank behind. "He was a loner," recalled Strain, for whom critical commentary comes only with difficulty. "He was not a good boss. He was not a good supervisor. He didn't delegate. He wasn't a good businessman. He just liked. . . mostly what he liked to do was to run a lathe. . . He was a hands-on, machine operator type."

No doubt more clear in retrospect than at the time, trouble was brewing. Frank's growing alienation from the company, Jesse's outright exit, and Doug's increasing equity, all combined to create a delicate moment in the life of the struggling BECO. With Doug doing the engineering and much of the cultivation of customers, and with Frank preferring to work in the machine shop, BECO needed a business manager. So it was that in June 1951, as Jesse left to resume his Air Force duties, Doug and Frank began their search for a new business manager. It took some time, but by the fall of 1951 they had identified their man: Don Frisbee. Strain had gotten to know Frisbee, partly through a mutual friend,

By the early 1950's Brown Electro-Measurements catalog boasted almost a dozen instruments, all built around the company's highly-successful line of impedance and resistance bridges.

John Gray, who had embarked on a chain saw business that would eventually grow into OMARK Industries. A clearly weary Strain related in a letter dated May 9, 1952, to Jesse Brown, things had not gone their way, and help could come none too soon:

> This situation was evident last fall but we have been unable to break loose any suitable man to take over some of the office load which has grown considerably with the rapid increase in the business. Don Frisbee, a young Harvard Business School graduate appeared to be our best prospect when we first got together with him last September. We proposed that he start with us on the first of January [1952] on a [stock] purchase arrangement. . . . The bank spiked our guns by moving him into a very responsible position in their trust department but we didn't give up and he has decided to go with us anyway and has given notice that he wants to be released as soon as possible which appears to be about June 15th. He will then be with us full time although he has put in quite a bit of time on weekends and evenings so far. . . .

Things took still longer than anticipated; it was not until September 29, 1952 that Frank Brown was able to notify the Oregon Corporation Commissioner that BECO had a new secretary/treasurer. It was a great relief to everyone to have Don Frisbee on board, for as Doug had noted in his letter to Jesse, "I have found myself worked into a corner and have not had adequate time to push the sales and development as it should have been." Things were looking up; Doug and Don were becoming good friends. They often car-pooled to work, since both men lived on the west side of Portland.

With the arrival of Don Frisbee the pace of daily management picked up dramatically. Here was a man of considerable skill and business acumen, who brought a new level of professionalism to the BECO operation. Gradually, however, it became apparent that he brought something else to the job: ambition. By the fall of 1952, as Frank Brown began to talk openly of his desire to get out of the business, the board – Brown, Strain and Frisbee – agreed that management personnel (that is, they, themselves) could purchase additional stock with their overtime pay. In practical terms this meant that Strain and Frisbee could purchase additional shares, since Brown had signaled his intention to disengage from BECO, a sentiment that became formal in February 1953, as noted in the Board Minutes.

Frank Brown's now openly-acknowledged desire to leave BECO precipitated a crisis. On the one hand, Doug Strain, the engineer at the center of BECO's modest success, had a vision for a company whose heart and soul would be dedicated to the production of the world's finest bridges, setting the standard for the measurement of capacitance and resistance that scientists and laboratories would look to the world over. Don Frisbee, on the other hand, with his business training and drive, believed that BECO should be more profitable, and that the shareholders of BECO should expect more generous returns on their investment. Thus, at the deepest level, Strain and Frisbee would never completely agree on the company's future. What mattered to Don — profitability — seemed to matter less to Doug. It was not that Doug did not take the business of business seriously, it was that Doug Strain was not, and would never be, driven by the desire to make money. Rather, his heart was in science and in the force for good that he believed science could be, and his vision guided him toward precision instruments, whose standards would be the bedrock on which science the world over could become that very force for good in which he so passionately believed.

As they kicked around the company's future throughout the spring of 1953, the two men continued about the business of running the company. Then, on July 7, 1953, things came undone.

ELECTRO-MEASUREMENTS, INC. 1953–1958

Brown Electro-Measurement Corp., 4312 SE Stark Street

The Storm Breaks

The spring of 1953 was unseasonably warm, as befit the thunderhead building above BECO, its board and its shareholders. During the first half of the year, despite tensions and overwork, the company moved to a new site. Having outgrown the confines of 4635 SE Hawthorne, BECO acquired somewhat larger accommodations in an altogether modest building at 4312 SE Stark St. "God, I remember that," recalled Armen Grossenbacher:

> That place was a cobwebby, dusty old place, and I remember going there on weekends and cleaning the place up prior to the move. I remember getting down in the cellar with a fire hose and just hosing it down. I remember going and painting... Well, in those days if you rented a building it wasn't like your landlord was going to fix it up for you. But it was a mansion compared to what he had [on Hawthorne]. We did have a basement, and we had a first floor , and we had a second floor.

In all, BECO's new quarters offered six thousand square feet, well over twice the space of the Hawthorne plant. The last two years had been relatively good. Profits approached $14,000 on gross sales of almost $100,000 each year. The company was paying down bank loans, and several personal notes. Things were still tight; the company was in no immediate financial danger. But the skies had begun to darken over 4312 SE Stark.

When at last, the lightning and its deafening thunderclap struck, on Tuesday, July 7, 1953, Doug Strain was taken off guard, not so much by the fact that differences existed among the company's three leaders, but by the sudden nature of the crisis. While Strain continued to carry the engineering and marketing functions of BECO that spring, a group of outside investors came together to bid for a change in leadership of the company. During late June and early July Doug was out of town. Upon Doug's return Monday the 6th, he was notified of a special meeting of the Board of Directors – Strain, Brown and Frisbee – for the morning of July 7.

At 7:00 am on the 7th, Doug Strain arrived at the meeting to be confronted with an ultimatum: he could either buy out the outside investors, or Doug himself would have to "step out." He had until Wednesday, July 15. It seemed impossible that in a week's time Doug Strain could come up with the cash to buy the company. Indeed, the outside investors felt confident that by the 15th they would be buying him out. As for the BECO employees, many felt very worried about the company's future. At least one, Armen Grossenbacher, stood with Doug. Others, however, seemed less sure of themselves.

The skeptics were in fact right: Doug Strain did not have the money to buy them out. Not in a day, not in a week, not in a year. What money he had, he had poured over the past several years into buying those shares that Frank and Jesse Brown had chosen to sell back to the company. Despite this investment, however, Doug was still not the majority shareholder. To make matters even more serious, BECO had tapped out its credit with the First National Bank, and the disinterest of other bankers left Strain no room to seek help from that quarter. By Thursday the 9th, Doug had spoken several times by telephone with his father Clayton. If he was going to try to buy the company, he needed capital now and in all likelihood a business manager very soon. Clayton Strain could offer both. As they talked, Clayton said he would be willing to come up from Los Angeles to be business manager of BECO, and, more to the immediate point, he was willing to put $25,000 into his son's company. So this was a start. But Doug needed more that $25,000 for the buy-out. As the clock ticked and his fund-raising options diminished one by one, Doug turned to the only friend who could help: Howard Vollum.

A Splendid Moment

Strain already knew of Vollum when the former arrived in Portland in 1949. As so many in the electronics industry would later recall, it was through a Tektronix oscilloscope that Strain first "met" Howard Vollum:

> I got acquainted with Tek at Beckman. I needed a scope badly for a special digital wavelength scale I was making for a new spectrophotometer. I needed to see it perform on a high-performance oscilloscope. [The Tek rep] brought in one of their first Model 511 demonstrator models…. The scope showed me what was going on, so I went to my boss and said, "I've learned as much in an hour as we've learned in six months on this project. We've got to keep this thing!" So when the rep came back that afternoon to pick it up so he could show it to somebody else, we all gathered around. And I said, "You're not taking that thing out of here. We'll fight you for it! We're going to use it for another week at least." And so we got to use the scope for another week and finish our project.

From his introduction to Tek scopes Strain developed a deep respect for the work that Vollum and his small company were doing. So when he came on board at Brown, he wasted little time in getting to know the Tek crew. The two companies, situated as they were about a mile apart on Hawthorne Blvd., made up the embryonic heart of what would become Oregon's high technology industry, what has later come to be known as the "Silicon Forest." And as "neighbors," Howard and Doug hit it off:

> We were just out on the street, you know, right out there on 47th and Hawthorne, and Howard used to drop in about, oh, once every two weeks, maybe once a month to see what was going on. And I was up there on 12th [and Hawthorne] at their operation raiding their inventory, bits and pieces, because we didn't – United Radio was doing its best to keep us supplied – but we didn't have any electronics stock in town. So [the Tek people] were coming down getting wire and stuff from us, trading back and forth, getting chits on each other. Everybody was around. Howard and Jack were very active, and I saw them once a week at least, maybe more often. Howard just came down, looked over our shoulder and asked the occasional question.

Doug Strain came to know Howard Vollum and Tektronix, the quality of Tek's instruments, the integrity of its owners and engineers. Thus it was, when he needed to cash in one of those old "chits," Doug Strain turned to Howard Vollum.

Ask Doug Strain to recall his conversation with Howard Vollum, and he will likely simply say, "Yah, Howard came through." And then Doug will try to change the subject. Because even today, almost half a century later, a closer retelling of that event moves Doug so deeply he has difficulty telling the story. Reeling from the shock of the ultimatum, Strain knew that if all else failed, "I could have gone back to Beckman." But he did not want to do that; his family was settled, and "I didn't want to just be whisked out." So as the shock wore off, after several sleepless nights, he turned to his Hawthorne Blvd. friend, Howard Vollum, arriving at Howard's house in the West Hills the evening of Friday, the 10th.

After a brief exchange of pleasantries, Howard could tell that something serious was on Doug's mind. Doug came quickly to the point, telling Howard, "I'm in trouble." As he related the events of the past several days and the details of the outside investors' ultimatum, Vollum became more animated. With his friend and partner Jack Murdock, Howard had just gone through the process of buying out the other three original shareholders of Tektronix, Milt Bave, Logan Belleville and Miles Tippery, and therefore had a very clear understanding of the difficulty of Doug's position and the need for decisive action. "What do you need, Doug?" asked Howard, whose directness often intimidated his own engineers, but which at this moment was just what Doug needed to hear. "I figure I need about $30,000, Howard," came the reply. At which point, Howard got up from the couch, and returned a moment later with his checkbook. On the spot Howard Vollum wrote Doug Strain a check. No discussion of collateral, not a word about when or how Doug would repay Howard. He simply wrote the check, saying, in the offhand way that so often characterized Howard's manner, "We'll work out the details later." And thus was precipitated one of those rare moments in the history of companies, a moment so characteristic of early high technology companies, and a moment especially characteristic of the altruism reflected in the lives of Oregon's earliest high-tech pioneers.

"Howard really came to my rescue," recalled Strain. Indeed he had. Now, armed with his father's $25,000 and Howard's check, Doug could face down the ultimatum. On

Monday the 13th, Strain called a shareholders meeting for the next day. Anticipating Strain's capitulation, the board was instead greeted on the 14th by Strain's $2500 check as a good faith sign that he would buy them out at $215 per share. In toto, Strain would pay $37,840 for the 176 outstanding shares of stock in BECO. Don Frisbee and Frank Brown sold their shares, acknowledging payment on July 19th and simultaneously resigning from the company and the board.

Throughout their careers, neither Doug Strain nor Howard Vollum were given to calling attention to their acts of kindness and generosity. So for Howard, his extraordinary act on behalf of a friend merited no mention to those who interviewed him over the years. Nor did he speak of what he did next. Doug began immediately to repay Howard's loan. A letter from Pope, Hewitt and Loback, Tektronix' accounting firm, dated December 23, 1953, certified that the remaining $21,500 was secured by 100 shares of BECO stock. Having no intent to profit personally from his private act, on September 14, 1954, Howard directed that the note be signed over to the Tektronix Employees Profit Sharing Trust.

The Cast Assembles

With the help of his father and Howard Vollum, Doug Strain had a company. Yet it threatened to be a hollow victory, unless he could put together a team that could build on the BECO foundation. By late July, Clayton Strain was on his way Portland, and in early August had taken up the reins as secretary and treasurer of the company. Clayton's very first move was to change banks, taking out a $30,000 line of credit with the Bank of California. For the moment, things seemed secure; Clayton Strain would manage the day-to-day operations, and Doug would look to the engineering and marketing. Much of the company's early success can be attributed to the contributions of Clayton Strain, whose friendly and understated style served the company well in his role as personnel manager, and whose financial expertise freed up his son for engineering new products and cultivating new customers. In many ways, Clayton Strain was the unsung hero of those very early years, having taken early retirement to play his quiet but crucial role in the success of the company.

Nevertheless, they were not out of the woods yet. There was simply too much to do, and too few employees to go around. Doug could not be everywhere, at all times, despite his valiant attempts. During his struggle to retain the company, he had sent Grossenbacher to represent BECO at the WESCON show, and while Armen acquitted himself well, they both knew they could not plug the dike like this forever. The company needed more engineers, and production management. And, while they were at it, the company needed a new name. By December things began to pick up.

First to arrive was Lawrence Rockwood. Back when Doug Strain was still at Beckman, and Rockwood was at Robinette, the two former classmates had lunch every now and then. Doug could tell that his friend was increasingly unhappy at Robinette. So he suggested that Rockwood look into an opening at Beckman, and sure enough, Rockwood got the job. Just as Doug headed north to join Frank and Jesse Brown, Rockwood arrived at Beckman. Within a year Beckman tapped Rockwood to be chief engineer. But things at Beckman were always chaotic, always changing at the top. In Rockwood's six years at Beckman he worked for eight different bosses; there seemed to

Clayton Strain, at his desk as General Manager of Electro Measurement, Inc. The wallpaper in the office on Stark St. did not last long.

be a revolving door at the top. Even though the company was growing rapidly, it just did not feel right to Rockwood.

Rockwood and his wife Vera liked camping, and took their vacations in the fall. In the fall of 1953 they came to Oregon to camp, to hike and to take photographs. On his swing through Oregon, Rockwood stopped in to see his friend, Doug Strain: "It was late fall and I went over to see him and we had lunch together, and he said, 'Why don't you come join me.'" It turned out to be an easier decision than Rockwood imagined: added to his dissatisfaction at Beckman was the fact that Rockwood's wife, Vera, was a Portland native. So, in December 1953 Rockwood agreed to join Doug as production manager, at $750 a month, plus an option to buy forty shares of stock.

The stock Rockwood optioned, by having $100 a month withheld from his paycheck, was no longer Brown Electro-Measurement stock. The day after Christmas 1953, Doug and Clayton Strain dropped "Brown" from the company's name, registering the company's new name with the State of Oregon, as Electro-Measurements, Inc. The spirit was good when Rockwood arrived: "Everything was going well, pretty good government contracts for the impedance bridge that Doug had redesigned, but Doug was trying to do too much...." It was clear, though, the company needed help on the manufacturing end of things:

Lawrence "Rocky" Rockwood, shortly after his arrival in Portland.

> When I arrived it was hand-to-mouth on manufactures. Doug would walk through with a notebook in his hand every morning and ask people: "what do you need today?" And then he'd get into the company station wagon and go downtown and buy parts that he could find locally. And then he'd go to the machine shop, which was a very crude little machine shop, and hack out some things that we might need right away. So there were obviously all kinds of stops and starts, as you'd try to make one thing, and have to set another aside, because you didn't have something else.

Strain had told Rockwood to "look around for a week and see what you want to do." "Well, obviously, when I watched what was going on," Rockwood recalled, "I could see they needed somebody that could run the manufacturing." The first thing he did was to call on the three key manufacturing employees: Armen Grossenbacher, Bob Elliott and John Healy. Together the four men began to rationalize the manufacturing process. As Rockwood, who came to be known at ESI as "Rocky," would recall years later:

> The first thing I did was went out and got a bunch of cheap paper and had the guys bring me all the parts on a quick-sketched picture and give each part a part number. They didn't have any part numbers or anything. There was no bill of materials. There was no way to explore the thing, or anything. So nobody really knew except by going and looking at the prototype, so that was the first thing I did for about two weeks to just get a bill of materials on all the various products....

A no-nonsense engineering manager, Rockwood's attention to detail quickly began to pay off. Those who fabricated parts began to standardize their work, those who assembled the instruments could rely on drawings and bills of materials, rather than having to eyeball a completed (or in some cases only partially completed) example. And service was easier, since with parts identified and numbered, it was easier to provide a replacement part.

Precision on SE Stark St.

Essentially, by 1954, Electro-Measurements, Inc. had four flagship products: the Model 250-C1 Impedance Bridge ($340), the Model 250-B1 Impedance Bridge ($295), the Model 850-B Amplifier ($60), and the Model 855-A1 Amplifier-Oscillator ($170). The bread and butter of the line were the impedance bridges. They featured exceptional accuracy, wide range, simplified operation, and the portability of a 9"x10"x10" box that weighed 17 pounds. The heart of the Electro-Measurements bridges was the unique "Dekastat," the secret of the outstanding accuracy of the Stark St. company's instruments. Electro-Measurement's literature explained: "Two coaxially mounted precision resistance decades in combination with an accurate interpolating rheostat provide a scale with more than 11,000 effective gradations and resolution of better than 1 part in 35,000. Overall accuracy of the unit is better than +0.05% of full scale." The Model 850 and the Model 855 were both peripherals, enabling customers to improve even further the accuracy and versatility of their bridges.

Even with such a limited line, the phenomenal accuracy of the Model 250 and the demand from industry and government kept the two dozen employees of the Stark St. plant plenty busy. If it was to expand its product line, what the company needed was additional engineering talent. And to fill this need, Doug Strain called once again on old friends. Merle Morgan, who stayed on at Cal Tech to pursue a graduate career, earned his PhD in Physics in April 1954. Doug had been in contact with Merle, hoping to bring his friend on board, and sure enough, upon graduation that spring Merle came to Electro-Measurements. In addition, Strain had hired his old friend from the war years, Harold Lawson, to act as Chief Engineer. Doug was intensely pleased that both men were part of the Electro-Measurements team, since in Lawson he knew he had an electronics pioneer and a man of virtually limitless practical knowledge, and with Morgan he had a scientific intellectual of the first order.

Another break was the arrival of George Vincent. Vincent was an engineer with an international reputation in calibration. For many years a mainstay at Eppley Labs in Southern California, Vincent was the chief architect of standard cells for primary voltage, and often referred to by engineers in reverent tones as "Mr. Voltage." As such, Vincent's reputation was enough to open doors at the National Bureau of Standards, as well as standards labs nationally and internationally. "Hiring George away from Eppley was a real coup" recalled Strain. "He really helped us get our foot in the door at standards and calibration labs at a crucial time in our development."

By 1955 Electro-Measurements was well settled into its quarters at 4312 SE Stark. The company numbered forty-six employees, nineteen women and twenty-seven men. Two small glass-enclosed offices on the ground floor housed the offices of Doug and Clayton Strain, a receptionist and a secretary. The rest of the building's two floors and basement were given over to engineering, manufacturing and shipping. The setting was intimate, everyone rubbed elbows, and everyone felt a sense of family. Shared restrooms led to pranks that often crossed whatever gossamer lines of rank and hierarchy that survived in such an open climate. This was a residential neighborhood, a storefront operation. And it attracted some attention from the neighbors; some just came in to look around, and some even landed a job. Years later, Elizabeth "Betty" Johnson recalled an afternoon in September 1955:

George Vincent, "Mr. Voltage," shown here in 1968 with a prototype high voltage measurement system intercomparison bridge.

After work at a wholesale grocery office, one evening, I drove by 4310 [sic] SE Stark on my way home, and as there was no name on this building, again my curiosity got the better of me, I stopped and curiously opened the front door. All was so quiet, but I noticed a particularly grey haired man bent over a desk in the right hand corner of the room. I knocked and he turned and said, "Come in." I explained that I was just one of the neighbors wondering what was going on in this building. He said, "Have a chair, we have others in this neighborhood who are wondering also." He was so pleasant to talk to. I told him my husband was ill and couldn't work, so I was looking for extra work. He told me, "You may be just the person we need, as their Mr. Rockwood needed help with the literature they mail out." So as fate would have it, I got the extra work. I was ever so pleased

I worked for Electro Measurements Inc. for about a year; liked the people and the company so much and asked Mr. Clayton Strain for steady work and got it. For some time I worked with the payroll, about 50 strong in those days, and helped Clayton Strain with the books.

The all-purpose front office of Electro-Measurements on Stark St. Doug Strain (left rear), Rocky Rockwood (center rear) and Clayton Strain (right rear), presided over the modest corner of the building.

Many employees took the bus to work. Those who drove parked on the street. At times, even cars were the object of pranks, as when a group raised the rear of Jack Burraston's car just a fraction off the pavement, so that no matter how hard he accelerated, the car could not move.

No one in the Stark St. plant could miss Jack Burraston. On June 27, 1951, Doug Strain had written to Jack, a long-time friend of his wife, who had lost his hearing but could read lips, to offer him an entry-level position:

> We believe we have a man-sized challenging job for you to tackle if you are interested in coming down here [from Seattle] to give it a whirl. We think it would be best to put the proposition on a 30 day trial basis so that we may both be certain that the job is mutually satisfactory.... If you are interested, hop the first train or bus down here and we will put you to work immediately... I think you will enjoy working with our gang of fellows.

Jack came, and although he started out in machine operation and assembly wiring, he soon found a more suitable niche: shipping. And from his domain, packing and shipping instruments, Jack would sing, sometimes well, other times not so well, but always at the top of his lungs. The strength of his voice matched the strength of his personality, since Jack believed that his was the final checkpoint for instruments leaving the company. Throughout his long career, Jack would carefully inspect the exterior of each instrument and then as often as not shake it. Any blemish, or any rattle, which of course he could feel but not hear, was cause to send the instrument back. Frequently, those to whom he returned the offending instrument were frustrated, but in the face of their objections, Jack would simply turn, and, hearing nothing, reading no lips, walk away.

Jack Burraston, whose unique presence enlivened and enriched two generations of the ESI family.

As Armen Grossenbacher had stood by Doug in 1953, so did Jack Burraston. And no one who ever met Jack could fail to recognize a true character when they saw him. Ask any ESI old-timer who stands out in their memory, and the first person to come to mind was Jack. And not just for his singing, or his fastidious inspection of instruments ready for shipping, but for his insistence on scrounging the packing boxes in which the company shipped its final product. Until well into the Macadam Ave. years, Jack Burraston insisted on purchasing the packing boxes from the cheapest source he could find. Thus, Electro-Measurements and later ESI instruments came to their customers in boxes bearing the printing and advertising of whatever odd lot or remaindered shipment Jack could buy from local box companies.

Only a few feet from the front office was the plant itself. On the ground floor, master machinists fabricated the mechanical parts, the chassis and the cases for all the instruments.

Upstairs, components came together painstakingly by hand, all soldered and individually tested by assembly personnel.

Also upstairs, was final assembly, where components, face-plates, dials and cases came together. From there instruments would go to "final check-out" with Jack Burraston before leaving the plant.

Happily, the shipments went out, out in increasing numbers. The years 1954 and 1955 saw steady growth in orders, sales, production and shipping. As early as the spring of 1954 these improving conditions produced several important decisions. Simultaneously, in April 1954 the board increased salaries and decided to inaugurate a profit-sharing plan. In the vast majority of cases, employees chose to take their salary increases in the purchase of stock options. This was a blessing to the company, and something the directors worked to encourage, since it meant that as the paper assets of employees accrued, Electro-Measurements could ease its cash-flow troubles just a bit. Additionally, it meant that from this point on, there would be pressure, at first ever so slight, for some concrete evaluation of the share value of the company's stock, even though it was not publicly traded.

As for profit-sharing, Doug and Clayton Strain unabashedly followed the model they saw working at Tektronix: a portion of net profits would be distributed among employees, part in cash and part put aside in a Profit Sharing Retirement Trust. Old-timers readily admit that as younger men and women they chafed at not receiving every nickel of their profit share in cash. Some even complained out loud at lunch, or in meetings. Armen Grossenbacher recalled: "Doug would say, 'I know, but you'll just have to trust me on this. Some day you'll thank me.' And, you know, he was right! If I'd have had it then, I would have just blown it on something like a new car. But now I've got it when I really need it and can enjoy it."

It was two and one-half years since he bought out his initial partners and Doug Strain could look back with considerable satisfaction. Business had doubled, and then doubled again, and they had moved from cramped quarters on SE Hawthorne Blvd. to the comparatively spacious accommodations on SE Stark St.. The number of employees had also doubled. The company's finances were on a solid basis. Electro-Measurements had inaugurated a profit-sharing program. And the company could boast of an exclusive customer list that included: The Atomic Energy Commission, Bendix, Boeing, Bonneville Power Administration, Cal Tech, Colgate Palmolive, Columbia University, Douglas Aircraft, Dupont, Eastman Kodak, Esso, Firestone Rubber, General Electric, General Motors, Hughes, IBM, International Harvester, L.M. Ericsson (Stockholm, Sweden), Lockheed, Martin Aircraft, MIT, National Bureau of Standards, National Institute of Health, National Research Council of Canada, North American Aviation, Pan American Airways, Pennsylvania Railroad, Phillips Petroleum, Princeton University, Republic Steel, Royal Swedish Army Board, Shell Oil, Stanford University, Standard Oil, Sylvania, Union Carbide, Union Pacific Railroad, U.S. Air Force, U.S. Army Signal Corps, U.S. Navy, University of California, University of Chicago, University of Michigan, Western Electric, Westinghouse, and Weyerhauser Timber. By 1955 it was clear that Electro-Measurements, Inc. was outgrowing its Stark St. location.

1956: A Vintage Year

During the waning months of 1955, the two Strains and Rockwood searched for a new building. Finally, rather than build their own building, they settled on leasing spacious new quarters in a building located at 7524 SW Macadam Ave., on the banks of the Willamette River in southwest Portland. The Macadam Ave. plant offered Electro-Measurements a total of 26,000 square feet, over 250% more room than the Stark St. plant.

In 1956 the entire Electro-Measurements gang took a break to gather out in front of 4312 SE Stark. In the front row, from right to left are: LeRoy Johnson, Lloyd Smith, Bud Callison, Bob Phillips, Jack Burraston, Jack Senn, John Richey, Armen Grossenbacher, Bob Long, and unidentified. In the second row, from right to left, John Van Wessem, Bob Elliott, Rocky Rockwood, Doug Strain, Clayton Strain, two unidentified men, Bobbie Abbott, Lou Huber, Jo Lukas, Ginnie Draper Sprague, Marge Ridens, Mabel Dennis, Jean Randle, Floyce Lee, Jessie Neff, unidentified, Eunice Martin, Cecelia Sattergren, Betty Johnson, Jessie Heisler, Mary Yeamans, Bill Greer, Predetta Glover, Merle Morgan, Ruth McGuire, John Healy, unidentified, Jack Riley, Jack Keene, Ward Philpott.

In the wonderful year 1956, the company's picnic was especially well attended, as families gathered in North Plains for softball, three-legged races, water-balloon toss, and the all-important hamburgers and hot dogs.

"If space gets short again soon," declared Doug in a progress report to the company's engineering sales representatives, "we can double our floor space once more by adding to the present building."

The move across the Willamette River took place in July of 1955, and was a company-wide team effort. Working overtime, evenings and weekends, the company was settled in by mid-summer and sent out invitations to friends and customers to visit the new plant:

> With a sense of pride we announce our move to a new and larger plant. Our new building has given all of us at Electro-Measurement a wonderful feeling of elation, like embarking on an exciting journey to new lands. But our sense of pride comes more from our work with you and your acceptance of

It was out the loading dock of 7524 SW Macadam
that Electro-Measurements, Inc. shipped "excellent
scientific instruments" by the fall of 1956.

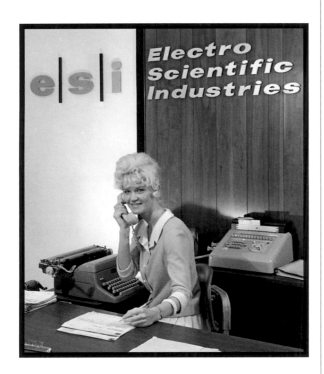

Inside the Macadam plant, visitors were greeted
by Nadine Jensen in reception. The offices of the
new plant were out front, affording much more
room for the management and administration
of Electro-Measurements' growing business.

our instruments. Your encouragement has given us the impetus to improve our offerings in the field of electronics and instrumentation. You, in a very real sense, are responsible for our move to our new building and to you we extend our sincere wish that you visit us soon at 7524 SW Macadam Avenue, Portland 1, Oregon.

Prominently displayed in large block type on the cover of the invitation were the letters "ESI." While nowhere on the invitation were these letters explained, the company's new stationery, which also bore the ESI logo, provided a clue. At the bottom of the page, in tiny letters, was printed: "Excellent Scientific Instruments."

Even before the move, new faces began to arrive. New engineers and technicians included Dick Booth, Tim Fleskes, Al Gotcher, Don Hazony, Bonnie Huddart, Eric Richardson, Jack Riley, Kenneth Sternes. Don Hoyt came on board as advertising manager, and Bob Pearson and John Bleth were hired to run the company's printing plant, complete with a full color press, a job press, and a multilith press. The printing plant was a reflection of the degree to which Electro-Measurements, and indeed much of American industry at the time, had become vertically integrated. A wood shop, a metal shop, welding booths, a paint shop, an anodizing shop, a print shop, all supported the central operations of engineering, assembly, test and shipping, that constituted the heart of the operation.

And what an operation it was! During 1956 Electro-Measurements' orders received increased by 61% over the previous year. Orders shipped increased by 59%. Personnel had grown by 38%, while at the same time Doug Strain calculated that per capita productivity had increased a remarkable 25%. The reason for such success was not hard to find: during the past two years Electro-Measurements had engineered a rapidly expanding product line whose performance really did merit the label "Excellent Scientific Instruments."

The backbone, the Model 250, still sold well, and was now accompanied by the Model 260 Comparison Bridge, the Model 270 Capacitance Bridge and the Model 290 Impedance Bridge. An increasing line of accessories enabled customers to expand the uses of their bridges. Of particular note was the Model 200 series Wheatstone Bridges. In addition, the early Dekapots had led to an entire component line: voltage dividers, or Dekapot Decade Potentiometers and Dekavider Decade Voltage Dividers; decade capacitors, known as Dekapacitors and Dekabox Decade Capacitors; and decade resistors, or Dekastats and Dekabox Decade Resistors. These were high-precision instruments, and they sold well. They required complex and precise windings, sometimes with unifiliar wire around a thin mica card, other times with non-inductive windings on a ceramic bobbin. In either case, windings were "trimmed" to the correct value in a painstaking process of sanding the surface of the coil until the exact value had been achieved.

Even as Electro-Measurements' engineers and designers worked to broaden the company's established lines, they began to venture into new areas. One such foray was into precision test equipment for synchro motors. Since for some time many of the company's Dekapots had gone into custom-built synchro test equipment, the engineers on Macadam designed a small compact Synchro Bridge for introduction at the 1957 IRE show. "We believe that this field of measurement suits our manufacturing techniques very well, as it is in both frequency and accuracy ranges with which we are familiar," Strain reported to his sales representatives.

There was another, more sophisticated reason that Electro-Measurements was interested in synchro test instruments: they had applications in the design and test of servo motors. Servo motors are high-speed, electric motors with exceptionally rapid on/off/acceleration rates that can position a piece of equipment or a component with great accuracy. And by 1956 Electro-Measurements was developing a new computer with special applications for servo system design.

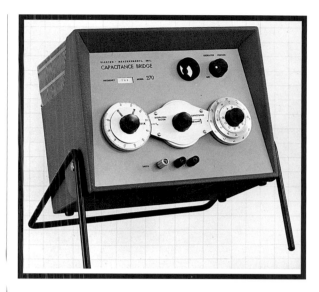

Merle Morgan's doctoral dissertation at Cal Tech, entitled "A Computer for Algebraic Functions of a Complex Variable," detailed his design and construction of a new concept in analog computer design. When he arrived at Electro-Measurements, he began to work intensively on refinements that would lead to the commercial production of this analog computer. Doug Strain referred to it as a "complex algebraic computer," when he discussed its development with potential customers and sales representatives in March of 1957:

> The basic electrical design on this unit is now well along, and we are pushing through the design details on the mechanical side. In addition to Merle Morgan's work on the Computer, Eric Richardson is spending full time on the mechanical design and Jack Riley... on error analysis and investigation of suitable materials for the resistive sheet required for the Computer.

He intended to have a prototype to demonstrate in the fall, either at the WESCON or the NEC show.

There was an undeniable air of optimism that permeated Electro-Measurement at the end of 1956 as employees celebrated their first Christmas on Macadam. The newsletter Jack Burraston worked so hard to put out carried Doug Strain's joyful message to his merry band:

> The year 1956 has been an important one in the growth of Electro-Measurements, Inc. We have moved into a new plant, which expanded our floor space by 300%, our sales have increased 50% our plant efficiency has increased 25%, and we have added new products, new personnel and a new group of foreign sales representatives.
>
> The management of ESI wants to take this opportunity to give warm thanks to all of you in and out of the plant, for your whole-hearted cooperation in improving the plant operation, and to our sales representatives for pushing our sales volume to a new high You have made 1956 the best year yet for ESI!
>
> 1956 has been a year of challenge and accomplishment, but even more rewarding has been the opportunity to work with each of you as individuals in achieving our common goals. Your friendly cooperation and interest has made the year a pleasurable one indeed!
>
> As we approach the holiday season, we would like to express our sincere appreciation by wishing each one of you A VERY MERRY CHRISTMAS AND A HAPPY NEW YEAR!

Electro-Measurements instruments had become famous for their ease of use. Engineered to be rugged and simple, the Model 270 Capacitance Bridge was so easy, even a monkey could use it, while Bill Lyon seems to have convinced Miss Syracuse that even she can operate the Model 291A Impedance Measuring System.

Looking back on this holiday greeting, one can sense the pride and satisfaction of a job well done and the buoyant optimism for the coming year. A closer reading also reveals the fact that in casual usage, people had begun to refer to Electro-Measurements as "ESI." Although it might mean "Excellent Scientific Instruments" at the bottom of the company's new stationery, no one knew just what it meant in this more casual context. It would be several years before they did.

By the spring of 1957 the gang on Macadam felt, if anything even more excited about the company's future. This spirit seemed to be captured in the arrival on April 1st of Charlie Davis, the fourth and final "horseman" in the establishment of the company. Doug Strain and Charlie Davis got to know one another as CO's at the Cascade Locks

The Model 250 Impedance Bridge, right, alongside the
Model 291 Universal Impedance Bridge, a system of
three rack-mount components: the Model 840R DC-
Generator Detector (top), the Model 860R AC Generator
Detector (center) and the Model 290R Impedance
Bridge. By the late 1950's, such systems had become
increasingly popular and would ultimately lead to the
ESI Calibration Console, a complete standards system
for the U.S. Air Force.

A young Charlie Davis, in the rarest of photos:
without a bow tie.

Wyeth camp in January 1942. Ultimately, the war took them in different directions.
Nevertheless, after the war Doug and Charlie stayed in touch. After the war Charlie
worked for some time with the American Friends Service Committee in Oakland,
California, and for a time with the Berkeley Co-Operative, before settling in 1949 in
Medford as chief accountant for a construction company. In 1953 he moved to Portland,
taking a position with Timber Structures, Inc. Timber Structures manufactured glue-lami-
nated trusses, beams, and arches, and had a management structure that Davis initially
found attractive. Ultimately, the company's accounting system, which Davis recalled as
"bizarre," attracted the attention of the IRS. Uncomfortable with Timber Structures' senior
management and its willingness to persist with a system that he and his colleagues
understood to be "manipulative," Davis decided to leave in early 1957.

When he had arrived in Portland in 1953, Charlie Davis resumed his friendship with
Doug Strain, at first in the Unitarian Church, but soon thereafter in a free-flowing discussion group known by its members as the "Splinter Group." The Splinter Group was a
loosely-constituted collection of some of Portland's most innovative businessmen and
futurists. Among the earliest members of the group were Jack Murdock, Don Ellis, and
Earl Scott, all from Tektronix, Doug Strain, and John Brookhart of the University of
Oregon Medical School. Because of the behaviorist bent of the group, a number of psy-
chologists and professors also attended, and the discussions had a profound influence on
the way that Murdock and Strain would manage their companies. Invited to come to the
bimonthly meetings of the Splinter Group, Charlie Davis once again came into contact
with Doug Strain. As the result of these contacts, Charlie turned to Doug in early 1957 to
ask if there might be a place for him at Electro-Measurements.

Doug Strain announced to the company that Charlie Davis was coming on board as
"personnel director and office manager." "He has had a great deal of practical as well as
college training in personnel and business administration," Strain continued. "His arrival
will release more time on the part of Larry Morin, Lawrie Rockwood, and myself for sales
and production liaison problems." In addition, Davis would assume some of the duties
of Clayton Strain, who, over the coming years, would gradually scale back his activities
with the company.

The Fire

Portlanders awoke on Friday, July 19, 1957, knowing that there had been a bad fire
somewhere in town, since engines from all over the city had been summoned. It was not
until the late editions of the *Oregon Journal* that readers learned that there had been not
one but two fires, one Thursday night and one Friday morning. The headlines that
gripped readers earlier in the day revealed that Miss U.S.A. was actually married and the
mother of two. Another headline screamed: "2 Hooded Men Beat Mother of Liberace.
Sedatives Required by Pianist." But by the afternoon, news of the two fires reached the
front pages: "Two spectacular Fires Hit Portland." Both were industrial fires, the smaller
blaze at the Screw Machine Products Company, the earlier and more disastrous fire at
Electro-Measurements, Inc. on Macadam Ave.

Ironically, as the *Oregon Journal* reported, both fires "provided unexpected activity
for scores of visiting firemen attending a convention here." Over five hundred fire chiefs

By mid-day on Friday, July 19, 1957, Portlanders learned the news of the Electro-Measurements fire.

were attending the Pacific Coast Inter-Mountain Association of Fire Chiefs, and fifty turned out to see how Portland's new Fire Chief, Harold E. Simpson, would handle his first big fire. In the end, Chief Simpson declared four alarms, involving eleven engine companies, two truck companies, two compressors and a first aid van. Two of Portland's fireboats also responded, but were of no use since the Electro-Measurements plant stood too far back from the Willamette River. The fire, which began just after 11:30 p.m. Thursday night, proved a stubborn challenge to the fire department, and was only brought under control after hours of difficult work.

Tragically, the fire never should have been more than a minor incident. But a series of mistakes and misunderstandings combined to turn an annoyance into a disaster. As part of the manufacture of its instruments, the company made its own resistors. At the end of the process, the resistors were baked in ovens that brought them to a high temperature and allowed them to cure, so that the resistors would not change value once they were installed in an instrument. At the end of the day on Thursday, July 18th, someone put a freshly varnished batch of resistors into the baking ovens to cure overnight. As the temperature rose in the ovens, gas from the fresh varnish blew open the door of one of the six ovens, expelling burning material onto a fresh pile of sweepings in front of the ovens, setting the sweepings on fire. The night custodian, himself a former fireman, immediately spotted the trouble, but instead of grabbing a fire extinguisher and putting the small fire out, he chose to run to the nearest fire box to call the fire in. Sadly, the fire box was two blocks from the plant, the man had trouble finding it, and when an engine did respond, it came to the box, not the plant. Valuable time had been lost, and more time slipped away as the firemen looked in vain for a fire adjacent to the call box. There was no one at the call box, because once he had called the fire in from the box, the night custodian returned to the plant to fight the fire, which by now was so smoky he could not re-enter the building.

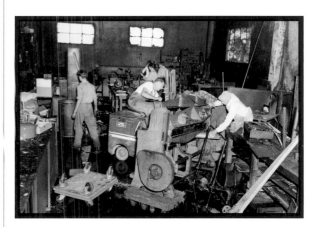

Armen Grossenbacher, who found his old chair somewhat intact, but little else, recalled that the first thing to do was to just "muck it out," as those from the metal shop did, shown here salvaging a sheet metal break.

Summoned from home, Doug Strain quickly arrived to find the fire department setting up to fight the fire from outside the building. Meanwhile, inside the concrete block building the contents of the plant were incinerated. "All our aluminum covers on all our instruments just evaporated. The tubes were little pools of glass on top of sockets...." Compounding the troubles was confusion over shutting off electrical power. The power company's failure to cut the power off quickly not only caused more trouble inside the plant, but it inhibited the firemen from working closer to the fire. In the end, unable to sort out which power company, Portland General Electric or Pacific Power & Light, was responsible for shutting off power, one of the firemen got a shotgun and shot out the fuse, cutting power to the plant. At the same time, Strain convinced the firemen at least to soak the wooden front office wing with spray, so that the company's records might be spared. The fire was stopped at the concrete wall that separated the office from the plant and the records were saved.

As onlookers trickled by, and later as employees showed up for work, they were greeted by a terrible scene. Up all night, having himself attempted to fight the fire, Doug Strain was a sight. The plant itself was a burned-out shell, save for the front offices. Typically, everyone pitched in. Betty Johnson "waded in 6 inches of water through the office to rescue my very important cash box containing the huge sum of $50.00." "There was nothing to do but to muck it out," recalled Armen Grossenbacher. No matter how willing to pitch in Grossenbacher and others were, things looked bleak that Friday morning. But by the end of the day, a variety of remarkable things combined to brighten Electro-Measurements' outlook.

Lloyds of London, Old Friends and Ironing Boards

Fortunately, the company had had the foresight to carry business interruption insurance with Lloyds of London. "I will give them a lot of credit," Doug Strain said many years later, "Their representative came out the next morning. We had about $70,000 of business interruption insurance, but we had to be out for thirty days before we'd get it. He looked at [the burned out plant] and said: 'This is going to be more than thirty days; here's your check.' I could have hugged the guy." The on-the-spot payment from Lloyds was immeasurable help to the company in meeting unfilled orders, as well as the new orders that continued to arrive.

Others pitched in as well. American Linen, which supplied the company with rags and cloth of all kinds, was johnny-on-the-spot the next day with thousands of rags and cleaning supplies to help with the cleanup. While Lloyds of London and American Linen had business relationships with Electro-Measurements, others who helped did so out of pure friendship. A neighbor several blocks down Macadam, offered garage space for Rocky and his crew to clean whatever machinery they could salvage. Another of Rockwood's contacts, Dean Child, had a very modern, well-equipped machine shop. Rather than unionize, Child had closed his shop. Seeing an opportunity to help, he offered to rent it to Electro-Measurements for $400 per month.

By far the most remarkable acts of kindness, however, came from Doug Strain's old friends Howard Vollum and Jack Murdock. On Friday morning July 19th, as word quickly made its way around the infant electronics community, Howard Vollum heard the news and instinctively knew just what to do. As Doug struggled to bear up under the strain that morning, Howard showed up. In his wake came half a dozen of Tek's big trucks. As it happened, Tektronix had just completed building a brand new warehouse. It was not open yet, but that did not deter Howard. In an act that still brings tears to Doug Strain's eyes,

> …Howard sent over an entire crew, with these low-bed trucks with trail-
> ers, to load all of our machinery. They hauled that machinery off to their brand
> new warehouse and proceeded on their own to strip the machines, rewind all
> the motors, repaint all the machines, put all the motors back and just rebuilt all
> our machinery. They never charged us a dime.

Electro-Measurements rented space in Tektronix' new warehouse for several months, by which time Rocky was able to relocate production to Dean Childs' shop and back to the Stark St. building, which, luckily, the company still owned.

Electro-Measurements had suffered a crippling blow. By Sunday, July 21st, the company put out a press release announcing that operations had been temporarily relocated, and that the complete resumption of production was expected within "45 to 60 days." "Plans for rebuilding the original plant site have been made. Re-occupancy of this plant will be possible in 90 days." Within days the company's machinery was up and running. Assembly was another matter. Rockwood's machine shops could manufacture some parts, but components and subassemblies were another matter. To handle this, as well as to keep their workforce together, Strain and Rocky ordered hundreds of Heath Kits, build-it-yourself kits for a wide variety of electronics equipment, available at electronics and hobby stores at the time. The women of the assembly operation came to the offices, saved from the fire and still operational at 7524 SW Macadam, to receive their Heath Kits, instructions and a soldering iron. Each woman then took her materials, and did her assembly work on her ironing board at home. "Cottage industry. I think we were able to give work to all our gals that wanted to continue."

There were delays, though. On July 29th the company conceded to its sales representatives that there would be a thirty to sixty day backlog. But by the end of September, things looked better. All of the insurance settlements had arrived contracts for the reconstruction of the plant were complete. "We have a promise of 60 days to complete the rebuilding job at S.W. Macadam," Strain reported on September 24th. He went on to describe the nature of the reconstruction, including air-conditioning, florescent lighting, filtered air, sound-proofing, tiled floors, and "Oh, yes, sprinklers! Don't forget the sprinklers over the entire plant. Make it fireproof and then water it down. 'BE PREPARED' is now our motto!"

The fire, so intense that it melted entire instruments into puddles of molten aluminum, copper, plastic and glass, confronted those who reported for work with a scene of utter devastation.

"Being prepared" included a full calendar of meetings, conferences and shows that autumn to assure at home and abroad that the company was well on its way to complete recovery. Assurances aside, however, since the fire things remained tenuous at best. As the result of the fire, gross operating profits sank from 8.2% in 1956 to 2.7% in 1957, and a low of 0.7% in 1958. The winter of 1957-1958 was especially difficult. While orders began to pick up by February 1958, shipments lagged at only 22.6% of the projected $190,000. Urging his employees to greater exertion, Strain tapped into everyone's frayed nerves around tax time: "We obviously have work to do or both Uncle Sam and ESI will go

The Dekaviders, Dekapacitors and
Dekaboxes were featured prominently
in the 1958 catalogue.

Here a technician at North American
Aviation uses ESI Dekapots in 1960 in
its C2-41M-A Flight Control
Alignment Console.

broke!" Still, the after-effects lasted for several years, as can be seen in a letter from a young Norm Morrison to his boss Merle Morgan, dated March 29, 1959:

> As the first anniversary of my employment with ESI approaches, I find it desirable to review my status with the company.
>
> You know, of course, some of the reasons I gave for wanting to work for ESI in the first place. It was not a big company, but had lots of promise. It had a good product line. Management was controlled from within and by engineering. The management and employees were friendly, cooperative people. The plant was located in Portland, near my family.
>
> I feel these are all still valid reasons why I would like to continue working with ESI. One big unknown factor in my first year with the company was whether or not my work would be satisfying… Now, have I enjoyed my job? At first, yes, although it seemed that projects did not terminate as quickly as I would have liked. The newness of the DEKATRAN development did much to keep the job satisfaction.
>
> Lately, however, the position has taken on elements which take most of the pleasure out of the work. There are just too many projects and so little time allotted to do them. If these projects didn't require so much time it would be different, but in my first year at ESI I have yet to see an "instant project." It is this supersonic pace and constant source of deadlines in product development work that have made up my mind regarding my future with the company.

Merle Morgan was able to assuage his young engineer's frustrations, and Norm Morrison remained at ESI for over twenty-eight years. Fire or no fire, though, the pace of work at ESI, as in any engineering-driven high technology company, often feels overwhelming.

In the final analysis, looking back on it forty years later, Doug Strain would say, "The fire came at a critical time in our growth. It really slowed us down, you know, over the next several years. It really did."

ELECTRO SCIENTIFIC INDUSTRIES INSTRUMENTS & OTHER POSSIBILITIES 1959–1969

ESI At Last

By March 1958 Electro-Measurements began to re-occupy its Macadam facility. Gradually, machines and equipment came back from their temporary homes at Dean Childs' workshop and the Stark St. plant. When at last the company threw open the doors to its new plant, Strain and Rocky were already talking of plans to add a second story to the 26,000 square-foot building. The grand re-opening of the Macadam plant was not the only cause for optimism. Even as they had mucked out and made plans after the fire, Strain, Rockwood, Morgan and Davis believed that the company's value was on the rise. On the day before Christmas 1957, acting as board members, the four had agreed that the price of Electro-Measurements stock would be fixed at $295.69 per share, up from an earlier book value of $215 per share. Their bullish view of the company's future, despite persistent difficulties raising new capital, was based on the research and development of Morgan and his engineers. Electro-Measurements was about to venture into new and promising territory with the appearance of a complete departure from its established instrument line: an analog computer. But would it do so as Electro-Measurements? Or as ESI?

For more than a year, verbally, and with increasing frequency in its written communications, Electro-Measurements had begun referring to itself as ESI. No longer just the tag line, "Excellent Scientific Instruments," the three letters, "ESI," began to appear as frequently as the words Electro-Measurements, Inc. The company seemed to be drifting away from its official name, and for an interesting reason. In 1958, Electro-Measurements, Inc. tried to register its initials, EMI, as its trademark, but ran afoul of the real EMI, Electric & Musical Industries, of Great Britain. So "EMI" was out. At the same time, "ESI" seemed to be gaining currency. At trade shows, the company banner highlighted Electro-MeasurementS, Inc. But if Electro-Measurements seemed to be losing ground, what would "ESI" stand for?

By 1959, company stationery bore both names, accented with a lightning bolt. Still, the letters "ESI" still did not stand for anything. Personnel in the accounting department complained to Clayton Strain that some customers refused to pay to "ESI," when the letters stood for nothing, since their own accountants balked at such an entry. It took awhile. Having ascertained that no international trademark conflicts existed with the letters "ESI," Strain and his team registered "ESI." Finally, they put "electro" and "scientific" together, settling on "Electro Scientific Industries," as words to fit the predetermined acronym. By the end of 1959, then, the company filed with the State of Oregon, making the name change to "ESI" official on December 29, 1959. By that time, however, stationery and catalogues already bore the more complete title: "Electro Scientific Industries," a name that in 1959 indicated the growing breadth of ESI's product line beyond just measurement instruments.

The various names under which the company has sailed, and the circuitous route that resulted in the final name of Electro Scientific Industries, have combined to confuse the issue as to the company's age. While a handful of strict-constructionists might insist that ESI dates only from its 1959 registration under that name, others have argued that ESI's roots originated in 1949, with the creation of Brown Electronics Company, under the partnership of brothers Frank and Jesse Brown and Doug Strain. BECO was, however, in reality the second incarnation of an earlier company, Brown Engineering Company, that was not merely the idea of Frank Brown, but in fact marked the first cooperation of Frank and Doug Strain in 1944. Assembling bridges under General Radio's contract with the War Department during World War II, Frank Brown and Doug Strain established the relationship that would lead to something special. By the spring of 1948, Doug and Frank had brainstormed new circuitry and a design that gave Brown Engineering something original to offer: the Model 250. Thus, the roots of ESI lie in 1944, in an event familiar to Northwesterners. Just as fire in the forest opens long dormant seeds, bringing new life to the forest floor, so, too, the fires of war in 1944 opened the seed of Brown Engineering, allowing the first seedling of the Silicon Forest to take root in Oregon, a seedling that would grow into the "First Electronics Company in Oregon," Electro Scientific Industries.

Piped-in-Music, Popcorn and Parking

What was it like working at ESI on SW Macadam Ave.? Well, first you had to get there. Traffic on Macadam could be formidable. The intersection in front of the plant, cars coming down the hill onto Macadam, commuters from the Sellwood Bridge, all combined to make getting to and from work a bit of a challenge. Once at work, however, the facilities made up for the hassle. The bright, well-lit, open work spaces, the well-equipped wood, sheet metal, machine and paint shops, and other amenities all created a

Bob Pailthorp, circa 1960.

great atmosphere. Management was interested in anything that would contribute to productivity. For a time, music was piped in over the PA system for fifteen-minute intervals, followed by fifteen minutes of silence. Joan Sulman and Hollis Smith, who had previously worked for Oregon Electric (OECO), or those who had worked for any of the area's metal shops, remember "that Macadam was just heaven as far as electronics companies."

Contributing to the atmosphere was the tradition of having free coffee and doughnuts in the morning. For years, and on into the Science Park days, ESI employees could partake of this daily treat, which helped create a very special working relationship among employees of all levels and functions. Bob Pailthorp, who as a student worked at the Macadam plant during his summers between years at Cal Tech from 1955 to 1959 and Stanford in 1960, and who started full time in 1960, recalled the Macadam plant "as a very pleasant place" to work:

> It was much more structured than it is now, in the sense that a bell rang in the plant for coffee breaks and lunch breaks. It came over the PA system. Everybody went to lunch or to coffee break together. I mean almost everybody in the company, except for somebody to answer a phone. And that was still true when we moved out here to [Science Park] Building I....
> A lot of good communication [happened] on those coffee breaks... All levels of the company were there and mixed and talked, and I remember talking to Charlie Davis a lot, or almost anybody.

Some things, however, did not change. Jack Burraston still ruled the shipping dock, and still scrounged for boxes. By now ESI made foam braces to buffer the corners of instruments when they were packed, but to cushion the instruments in their boxes Burraston and his crew used popcorn, poured from huge industrial-sized bags. Bags and bags of popcorn. "I remember the popcorn," said Strain with a wry smile:

> Westinghouse was an especially good customer and one day we got an urgent call from Westinghouse for some spare parts. They were shipped the same day, packed in popcorn. A note came back saying, "Thanks for the fast service. But I did not expect to receive my lunch, too!"

The popcorn worked well, but eventually caused a rodent problem at the plant. One person who particularly appreciated the popcorn, at least at first, was Joan Sulman:

> What was really neat was that you could walk down to the [Willamette River] waterfront and onto the dock and feed the ducks. [Shipping] made this marvelous discovery about packing material. They could use popcorn for packing material, and we would take some popcorn with us and go down and feed the ducks. It wasn't until we found out they had started putting rat poison in the popcorn that we figured out it wasn't....

Another thing that had not changed since before the fire, since Stark St. in fact, was the parking problem. As ESI grew, parking became scarce. Indeed, to those charged with conceiving of future growth, parking became a limit to growth. Rockwood and Strain might imagine building a second story on the plant, but the City of Portland would have none of it unless the company provided additional parking.

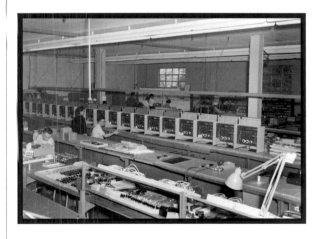

The re-built plant, with more light, better use of space, and a built-in sprinkler system, came back on line in the spring of 1958. The order backlog was tremendous, evidence of which can be seen in the nineteen Model 291 Universal Impedance Bridges waiting for final check-out (bottom).

Engineering for the Future

While there seemed to be physical limitations to growth by the early 1960's, new engineering and new products told another story. With the Cold War at its zenith, and

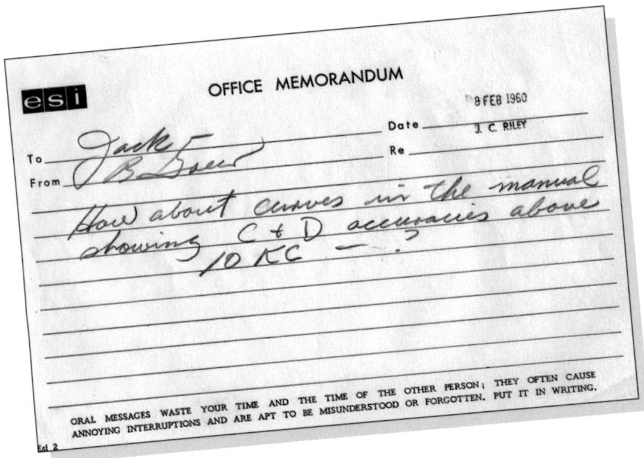

OFFICE MEMORANDUM

(handwritten memo)

8 FEB 1960

Date _____ J. C. RILEY

To _____ Jack Green

From _____ JB Green

How about curves in the manual
showing C + D accuracies above
10 KC —

ORAL MESSAGES WASTE YOUR TIME AND THE TIME OF THE OTHER PERSON; THEY OFTEN CAUSE
ANNOYING INTERRUPTIONS AND ARE APT TO BE MISUNDERSTOOD OR FORGOTTEN. PUT IT IN WRITING.

With the crush of business, Charlie Davis tried everything he could think of to facilitate productivity, including office memorandum forms that read at the bottom: "Oral messages waste your time and the time of the other person; they often cause annoying interruptions and are apt to be misunderstood or forgotten. Put it in writing."

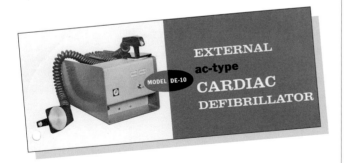

EXTERNAL
ac-type
CARDIAC
DEFIBRILLATOR

MODEL DE-10

ESI's short-lived cardiac defibrillator.

with the Kennedy Administration's inauguration of the "space race," demand for ESI instruments was at an all-time high. ESI's reputation for quality, its attention to detail and its commitment to service created a complete package that attracted customers. Some were taken with ESI's individually engraved face plates, others to the company's ability to meet unusual specifications. While some instrument cases – "boxes" – were still made of mahogany, other boxes were metal, finished in the characteristic brown or gray "crackle" of baked enamel on metal. But when a customer, the U.S. Navy, for instance, wanted a different box, ESI was quick to respond. Bob Pailthorp recalled the case of the Model SR104 Standard Resistor ordered by the Navy:

> … standards were in mahogany boxes at that time, and we didn't want to use wood. You know, Formica seemed like a better, more durable choice, and we found a company back in Maine or somewhere that made boxes that would meet Navy shipboard standards for ruggedness and so forth. When it came time to specify the Formica for this box, I decided if there's anything I didn't want, it was something that looked like a mahogany box. So I specified white Formica, and it's still built by TEGAM [to whom ESI sold its instrument division in 1994] the same way….
>
> It became a kind of unique identifier. Every time you walked in the lab and you could find a white box, you knew what it was.

Work with the government was a staple of ESI's business, and over the years the company had little difficulty meeting military requirements, whether technical specifications, the way the instrument was packaged, or even the type of shipping containers required by the military. Military inspectors routinely visited the plant and were on good terms with ESI personnel. Occasionally, though, something came up, as Pailthorp recalled with a shipment of bridges to the Navy:

> We did enough business with the Navy that there was a Navy inspector who regularly came to the plant, and mostly just checked to make sure the paperwork was OK, but he would physically look at the instruments and so forth. One time there was a small shipment to go, and a different inspector showed up, because the regular guy was on vacation. Someone in the Navy Department saw "bridges," and sent a guy who inspected highway bridges and boilers. So in this case all he did was to look at the paperwork….

By the late 1950's inspectors and clients who visited the plant, and customers who came to ESI's booth at shows learned that the gang at Macadam was ready to roll out two new products. Realizing that ESI's product line, while world-class in terms of quality and performance, had a limited future market, engineering sought new products that would bring ESI new markets. And the company had an open mind. Briefly, ESI ventured into medical devices, working with surgeons at the University of Oregon Medical School to design and manufacture a heart defibrillator. This was technology that matched up nicely with ESI's expertise, since for a heart defibrillator to work the current applied to the heart must be limited. "All you've got to do," recalled Strain, "was to get a high impedance source for the current… You get limited current through the [heart muscle] tissue, but we used higher voltage and a much lower current to limit tissue damage." Eventually, ESI made several hundred defibrillators, not only for the University of Oregon Medical School, but for the Veterans Administration Hospitals as well. But this venture did not last long. The possibility of product liability litigation cooled the company's ardor for its new device. "One suit would ruin you," said Strain, "and I was getting phone calls in the middle of the night from the doctors, saying, 'Your defibrillator isn't working right and we've got an emergency here. It's not working!' And I'd ask, 'Well, sir, have you plugged it in?' 'Oh, does it have to be plugged in?!' Anyway, we decided that we just couldn't stand that, so we deliberately dropped out."

ESIAC

As fleeting as ESI's venture into defibrillators had been, its entry into two other new areas was in earnest. The first of these initiatives was based on Merle Morgan's doctoral work at Cal Tech. Morgan had designed and built a unique analog computer that could quickly solve complex Laplace transform equations. When he arrived at Electro-Measurements, among his projects was an all-out effort to design and market a commercially viable version of his computer. Even as Morgan completed his graduate work at Cal Tech, the computer began to emerge from its murky origins in World War II. Individual, purpose-built computers, such as the Colossus Mark I and Mark II helped Allied codebreakers crack German signals During the war the U.S. Army contracted for the construction of a master computer that could plot ballistics trajectories for the mathematical tables used by artillery men in the field. Although the war ended before the computer was completed, the work was not in vain, and in 1945 Howard Aiken's Electronic Numerical Integrator and Computer, or ENIAC, became operational. Refinements followed and in 1951, the Sperry Universal Automatic Computer, or UNIVAC, was delivered to the U.S. Census Bureau. By the mid-1950's a score of other companies had entered the fray: Marconi, Ferranti, English Electric, the British Tabulating Machine Company, EMI, Plessey, Elliott Automation Ltd., Leo Computers, and Powers, Samas Accounting Machines Ltd. A late entrant, IBM, did not really become an active competitor until the end of the 1950's. In most cases, these companies developed computers to handle the brute force computational problems of statistics, accounting and basic calculation, since, after all, these were the most promising commercial applications. But there were areas of science and engineering that demanded more complex calculations using Laplace transform equations. And these were areas of great strategic industrial importance.

Bell Labs, and a handful of other research centers, concerned themselves with the arcane problems of plotting dynamic equations using Laplace transform analysis and known as "root locus" plots. This was critical work for aerospace designers and engineers who worked on the baffling problems of airflow, vibration, and the structural integrity of airframes on jet airplanes and rockets. By the late 1950's Bell Labs had invented an analog modeling process to study Laplace transform equations by using electrolytic tanks, with flexible metal surfaces covered with magnetic filings. When probes applied current in a predetermined fashion to the metal surface the magnetic filings would form in patterns that would yield a solution to the problem under scrutiny.

Merle Morgan had a better idea. Ultimately based on five patents, Morgan and his team designed and built an analog computer that could plot Laplace transform equations, on a logarithmic plot of the "S" plane. He believed that he could satisfy the boundary conditions of such a plot electrically, by means of a resistive sheet of paper, on which the boundary conditions were satisfied mathematically on the log "S" planes by putting constant potentials on the edges of the conductive sheet. Once the conductive sheet was

The Model 10 ESIAC Computer. "When I showed one to Werner von Braun," recalled Doug Strain, "he was so excited he ordered ten right on the spot for all his engineers in Huntsville, Houston and White Sands."

Doug Strain demonstrating the ESIAC
at the NEC show in 1960.

Paul Lintner (left) and Ed Swenson (right) both cut
their teeth at ESI marketing the ESIAC. Lintner went
on to Mikros to market the electron microscope,
while Swenson continued to work with Merle
Morgan on the ESIAC.

in place, instead of plotting poles and zeroes, Morgan's computer would move electric probes that would pick up the voltage around the sheet. Taking half a dozen poles, the computer would sum their currents and find the solution: the final curve. Rather than using metal sheets and magnetic filings, Morgan used carbon-impregnated Teledeltos conductive paper, the same paper that ESI had used for the printouts on its defibrillators. By summing the various voltages the probes picked up running across the Teledeltos paper, Morgan's computer gave solutions to Laplace transforms, one of the most complex calculations in mathematics.

By late 1957, Morgan was ready to demonstrate his computer. But what to name it? Without much ado, the die was cast: if there was an ENIAC, and there were UNIVACs, ESI's analog computer would be the Electro Scientific Industries Analog Computer, or ESIAC. The ESIAC Model 10 came on the market in March of 1958. It was an almost instantaneous hit with both industry and government. Aerospace contractors, bedeviled by the uncontrollable vibrations of airframe components subjected the stresses of huge jet engines, particularly those used in the U.S. Airforce's ICBMs, were delighted to find that the ESIAC solved all sorts of problems. In fact, Werner von Braun was so impressed with what the ESIAC could do for his rocketeers that he bought a brace of them, one for each of his key design engineers at NASA.

Many ESIAC customers were in the defense-related industrial sector. But Boeing, one of the company's most enthusiastic customers, put the ESIAC to use solving key design problems on commercial aircraft. Having experienced such success with its long-range 707 passenger jet, the Boeing Company was hard at work developing the next generation intermediate range passenger craft, the 727. The 727's design offered unique challenges to Boeing's chief 727 engineer, Lembit Kasenkranius, stemming from the plan to mount the airplane's engines in the tail of the aircraft. Early pre-flight calculations and modeling indicated that the plane would not be airworthy. But once the ESIAC arrived, new pre-flight equations solved the problem within days.

Morgan and his troops had every right to feel elated. With the help of several young assistants, Paul Lintner in marketing and his chief applications engineer, Ed Swenson, Morgan's computer sold well between 1959 and 1963. And Merle worked hard to insure the computer's acceptance within the academic community. He published continuously in academic and technical journals, explaining and extolling the virtues of the ESIAC. He and Ed Swenson teamed up with one of the nation's leading experts on computers, Professor Otto J.M. Smith at Berkeley, writing more papers. But acceptance at the university level eluded the ESIAC. In 1966, near the end of the ESIAC program, the list of university laboratories with an ESIAC was short indeed: Berkeley, City College of New York, Cornell, Louisiana Polytechnic, Portland State University, Oregon State University and the University of Brazil in Sao Paulo.

What was the problem? Why, in the end, were fewer than four dozen ESIACs sold? For one thing, engineers who seemed so enamored of the ESIAC solved their initial problems quickly with the computer and then seemed to put it aside. At $10,000 a copy, the ESIAC did not represent that great an investment for major corporate customers, and certainly a small ticket for the government. Rather, industry and government were making a much greater investment in digital computers. Thus, the pressure to amortize their investment in digital mainframe systems meant that ESI's customers forsook analog for digital; by 1965, RCA, NCR, Burroughs, Univac, IBM, Honeywell, Philco and Control Data had captured the market in scientific and industrial computer applications. By the late Sixties Digital Equipment, Hewlett-Packard and Data General had also joined the battle. By 1966, it was time for ESI to bow out of the computer wars.

Mikros

In 1960, as the future of the ESIAC looked bright, ESI prepared to launch another new venture. Out in Forest Grove where Doug Strain happened to live, at his daughter Barbara's alma mater, Pacific University, a young physicist, Dr. Gertrud Rempfer, was experimenting with electrostatic lenses. Professor Rempfer had a precocious student, Tom Holce, who worked with Professor Rempfer on her experiments. Gertrud Rempfer brought to her work a passion for precision, complexity and exactitude characteristic of her Swiss background. Tom Holce, on the other hand, possessed a practical streak that made him somewhat impatient with his fastidious professor.

Tom Holce graduated from Pacific University in 1958, staying on as an assistant to Dr. Rempfer to work on a project Rempfer was doing for Motorola on electrostatic, short-coupled TV tubes. In the spring of 1959, Holce completed a prototype of his electrostatic electron microscope, a simple, rugged instrument that was not only fast, it was easy to maintain. At that time, the state-of-the-art electron microscopes, made by RCA, GE and Phillips, used electromagnetic lenses. The essential difference between the electromagnetic and the electrostatic lens was one of intensity. Both focused a beam of electrons on a target. The electromagnetic beam was a very high voltage, intense beam of at least 75 to 100 kilovolts, whose very intensity could, and did, burn up its target. The electrostatic beam required only a fraction of the power, roughly 10 kilovolts. That made it cheaper and cooler to operate, and it left the target intact.

Tom Holce knew Doug Strain, and approached Doug with the proposal that ESI take on Holce and manufacture his microscope. In August of 1959, ESI hired Tom Holce to head an engineering group to produce the electrostatic electron microscope. And what Holce and ESI soon discovered was that since the beam was so much less intense, and since it did not burn up the target object, they could look at things like cotton fibers or electrolytic carbon without vaporizing them

Realizing they had a potential winner on their hands, Strain, Morgan, Rockwood and Davis not only brought Holce into the company, they decided to set up a subsidiary for the production of electron microscopes. Holce would do the engineering. For marketing, they chose Paul Lintner, who had done so well getting the ESIAC off the ground, and to manage the company on a day-to-day basis Larry Morin came over from ESI. All three would have an interest in the new company, christened on April 13, 1961 as Mikros.

The Mikros electron microscope enjoyed considerable success. While the RCA, GE and Phillips electromagnetic electron microscopes began at between $30,000 and $50,000, the Mikros electrostatic electron microscope was much cheaper, at $15,000 per copy. Lenses and other peripherals added to the cost, bringing the system to roughly $25,000. This was still a dramatic saving over the electromagnetic microscope. In addition, Mikros manufactured a line of vacuum evaporators and vacuum gages, in what *The*

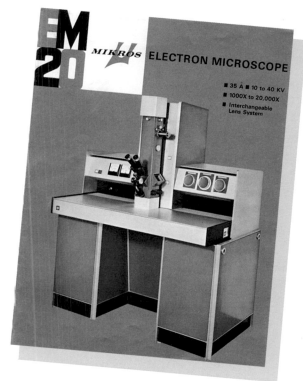

The Mikros Electron Microscope.

Tom Holce (right), who developed the Mikros electron microscope, enjoying a moment with Al Rosen.

John Elorriaga, seen here in later years as an ESI Board member, whose tour of the Macadam plant with Clayton Strain in 1960 proved critical to the growth of the company.

Groundbreaking for Science Park began with the ignition of an explosive charge, triggered by a tone signal from the U.S. Bureau of Standards, activated by Governor Mark Hatfield (right) who initiated the signal with an ESI Model 292 Capacitance Bridge. Looking on, from right to left, were: Dr. Edward Creutz, Director of Johns Hopkins Laboratory for Pure Science; Dr. Lee Lusted, head of the Physical Sciences Division of the Oregon Primate Research Center; Doug Strain; and John Gray.

Oregonian's business editor, Gerry Pratt, described as "an operation where they manufacture exotic $15,000 electronic microscopes and vacuum systems that only the technicians of the electronics industry really understand." Within a relatively short time, however, the under-capitalized Mikros found its competition came not from the established U.S. electron microscope companies, but from across the Pacific. Cheaper Japanese electron microscopes, particularly at the electrostatic low end of the business, simply undercut Mikros. In June of 1965, ESI sold Mikros to Varian for $750,000. Part of the agreement called for both Holce and Lintner to go to Varian with the Mikros business unit. Neither Holce nor Lintner found relocating to Varian's California operation to his liking. In the end, both men took their equity from Mikros. Holce struck out on his own, becoming one of Oregon's most successful entrepreneurs; Lintner returned in 1966 to ESI.

Finances and Science Park

The move into new products, and the cost of rebuilding ESI's base during the years after the fire, brought new financial pressures, pressures that Clayton Strain and Charlie Davis found difficult to overcome with the help of the Bank of California. From the late 1950's on, Doug Strain would complain openly, sometimes even bitterly, that Oregon was hardly fertile ground for investment in exotic electronics developments like the ESIAC or Mikros. "So far," Strain commented to *The Oregonian* in December 1964, "we have not found a nickel of equity capital for this type of thing in Oregon." It was precisely this problem that led ESI to seek out Varian to take over Mikros. So as early as 1960, it was clear that ESI would have to find a different bank. Thus began a process that would culminate in ESI moving its accounts to the U.S. National Bank, in Portland, Oregon.

The history of the early days of high technology in the United States is littered with the remains of fledgling companies that died for lack of adequate funding. Essentially conservative, bankers have not been known for their risk-taking when it comes to businesses they do not understand. Many of the most successful high technology companies in the Forties and Fifties had to boot-strap their own capital. Some even resorted to accounting practices that minimized their taxes by shifting inventory from one year to another. Even when the IRS objected, paying penalty and interest fees was cheaper than paying bank rates.

Unable to boot-strap additional funds, ESI preferred to stick with its bankers, and a handful of individual investors, rather than resort to less orthodox methods. But it had become more and more difficult to increase the company's line of credit with the Bank of California. In the spring of 1960 ESI approached the U.S. National Bank, whose initial reaction was cool at best. But Clayton Strain and Charlie Davis persevered, however, opening an account with the bank and applying for a line of credit. Eventually, perhaps as much to get rid of their pestering client as service it, the U.S. Bank sent a new young loan officer, John Elorriaga, out to Macadam Ave. to look ESI over. Clayton Strain greeted Elorriaga when he arrived. They talked for a bit, and then the elder Strain asked him if he would like a tour of the plant:

> … they wanted me to go out and look at the plant. So I went out there and went through the plant. They had the ESIAC then, and of course I didn't understand that. In fact, I didn't understand anything. I went through the plant and then I came back. And I asked my boss, Charlie Harding, who was a vice-

president on the executive committee of the bank and who had turned the account over to me, "Do you want me to put in the file what I really know about the company?" And he said, "Yes." So I wrote in the file that the only thing I understood about this company are the "Exit" signs above the doors. But I found there the most wonderful people you can imagine, just 100 percent honest, true, hard-working, smart, believable, just wonderful, wonderful people....

So we went along, and I was loaning them money on nuts and bolts, you know. The banks don't do that very often, but we were because we thought so much of them....

So on August 5, 1960 ESI moved all of its accounts to the U.S. Bank, taking out a $200,000 line of credit. Part of the bank's agreement with ESI required calculating anew the value of the company's stock. By April 1961 the board placed a value of $462.07 per share, valuing the company at just under $2 million. With the new infusion of capital, the instrument line, the ESIAC selling well, and the electron microscope on the horizon, Rockwood and Davis began to study plans for adding a second story to the Macadam plant. Within months it became apparent that adding a second floor was not in the cards, since the City of Portland demanded more parking than ESI was willing to build.

ESI could not long postpone its need for additional space. The board began to look for suitable property, and over this issue there is little doubt that Doug Strain's utopian outlook influenced the final choice. By February 1962 the directors had spotted a parcel of some 170 acres between the Sunset Highway and Cornell Road. Strain and his colleagues liked the idea of moving west of Portland in Washington County, settling in an area that Tektronix had already made fashionable. Strain had a vision of a science park, on the order of the highly successful Hewlett-Packard Science Park in Palo Alto, California. Furthermore, Washington County planners indicated that a new Fred Meyer retail store was going in adjacent to the parcel, and would serve the residential neighborhood that had sprung up to the north of Cornell Road. In Doug Strain's vision, the employees from the various companies located in his new Sunset Science Park would live in the neighborhood, walk to work, and shop right there.

Vision and reality seldom mesh perfectly. ESI could afford only 70 acres, so Strain lined up his old friend John Gray to invest in the other 100 acres. Eventually the Fred Meyer deal fell through, and John Gray sold off his land in smaller parcels. In the end, Merle Morgan was the only ESI employee to buy a house within walking distance of the company's new plant.

By the end of 1962 ground was broken for the first of a planned three-building campus for ESI in the Sunset Science Park. Construction went well, and by March 1963 the foundation and concrete slab floor for the first building were complete. From this point on, observers of the blueprints of the architects Broome, Selig & Oringdolf could tell that something unusual was under construction. On the completed slab floor workers built thirty-six T-shaped forms, at intervals around the edge of the floor. Into these forms came rebar and then concrete, making custom-built interlocking pilasters. And on April 15th, each of the thirty-six pilasters was tilted up and into position, creating the skeleton of the four walls of the building. Re-enforced steel joists, roof-decking and cedar siding completed the exterior of the building. Christened Building I, the 20,000 square foot structure had no windows, for it would use the heat from internal lighting fixtures in the winter, and an air-conditioning system in the summer. Climate control was crucial, since

Sunset Science Park, winter 1962-3, 75 acres of farm land that became ESI's new home. Looking north, the dark building in the center of the picture is Sunset High School. To the south of the Sunset campus, the gentle sweep of Science Park Drive can be seen, running from Murray Road on the east, to Cornell Road at its northwest terminus. To the south of Science Park Dr. is Highway 26, whose separated lanes reach only as far as the foundations of ESI's Building I, the white rectangle between Hwy. 26 and Sunset High School.

Construction of Building I proceeded quite rapidly, using interlocking concrete "T" shaped pilasters to create the framework of the building.

The completed Building I in the
fall of 1963.

the engineering and final calibration of instruments required very precise temperature control, in particular to meet military specifications. Therefore, inside a series of internal rooms, temperature was stabilized to one-100th of a degree. Since the heat given off by an average person equaled that given off by a 50-watt light bulb, each room had a number of 50-watt bulbs burning. Each person entering the room would turn off a bulb; upon exiting, the bulb was turned back on, thereby holding the temperature steady.

Building I attracted a good deal of attention. Its design, basically a shell within a shell, its temperature-controlled environment, and the absence of any windows were all radical for its day. Employees did not seem to mind the lack of windows, or at least they did not complain. Rockwood and Strain did a good job of explaining that sunlight coming through glass windows would produce temperature variations that would be difficult to control. Eventually, however, windows did appear, as it became easier to control the atmosphere within the interior test rooms, and as a concession to those working in the rest of the building.

First to occupy Building I were the administrative, marketing, engineering and technical services departments. The company retained its Macadam facility, where there was more space for manufacturing and the various shops that served engineering and manufacturing. Not until several years later, when Building II came on line at Sunset Science Park did manufacturing and the shops vacate the Macadam facility. Meanwhile, as plans for Building II began to take shape, plans developed to move Mikros from its quarters on SW Capitol Highway to a new building in Sunset Science Park. In each case, the ESI board structured the buildings' finances through the ESI Profit Sharing Trust. The buildings were owned by the Profit Sharing Trust, and leased back to ESI. This arrangement would last a number of years, but eventually with the change in pension regulations the company would buy its buildings from the Trust.

Sunset Science Park was clearly central to Strain's and ESI's vision for the growth of high technology in Oregon. Brochures and trade articles touting Science Park, emphasized the dual presence of ESI and Tektronix in Beaverton, the convenience of Highway 26, Oregon's clean environment and the fact that "within a ten mile radius there are seven colleges and universities to support technical work at the Park." But it came too soon. ESI remained the Park's single tenant of substance. When Varian bought Mikros they remained for several years in the Science Park location, but eventually Varian moved its operation to California. ESI is still the Park's anchor tenant, accompanied by others, such as ADC Kentrox, founded by Tom Holce. The concept of a science park has become a reality, however, in a more diverse and heterogeneous form. As companies have spun off from Tektronix and ESI, and as scores of others from around the country and overseas have established operations in Washington County, the "Silicon Forest" has taken root and flourished. Even the educational vision that Strain worked so hard to foster has come alive, with the establishment of the Oregon Graduate Center (ultimately Oregon Graduate Institute), and later the Lintner Center.

What Next?

By 1966 ESI was back to its traditional product line. The ESIAC had run its course, the electron microscope sold off at a profit, albeit a modest one. In 1966 ESI's earnings were $160,000 on gross sales of $2,333,126. And although ESI's newest addition to Sunset Science park, Building II, was complete and manufacturing successfully moved in over the Labor Day weekend of 1966, the fresh breezes of years past seemed to have slackened. In 1967, profits fell off, in what senior management attributed to "the costs of the move, development costs for new models, and manufacturing costs." They nevertheless took comfort in the fact that ESI ranked very highly versus top ten companies in the field in terms of average five-year return on investment:

1.	Tektronix	19.9%
2.	Hewlett-Packard	17.0%
	(ESI	**16.8%)**
3.	Wallace & Tiernan	14.6%
4.	Veeder Industries	13.2%
5.	Rockwell Mfg. Co.	13.0%
6.	Taylor Instruments	12.8%
7.	Gulton Industries	12.8%
8.	Itek	12.7%
9.	Becton Dickinson	12.6%
10.	Perkin-Elmer	10.9%

Even ranked against some of the country's most prestigious companies, ESI came off well in this five-year average:

Polaroid	26.0%
Xerox	25.1%
Eastman Kodak	21.4%
IBM	17.0%
(ESI	**16.8%)**
Textron	16.7%
Litton	16.4%
TRW	14.5%
Ling Temco	13.9%
Burroughs	14.2%
Pitney Bowes	12.0%
Bell & Howell	11.7%

If ESI board members took comfort in these data, by 1968 it was cold comfort indeed. Paul Lintner returned to ESI in 1966 and his energetic efforts as vice-president for marketing included expanding ESI's presence to the East Coast, with offices in Massachusetts by the end of 1968. Still, the results were modest.

As soon as spring arrived in 1964, ESI had a sales meeting to show off its new headquarters. Front row (left to right): Dan Bell, John Healy, Dick Espejo, Bill Lyon, Bill Greer, Tom White, Stan Gressel. Back row (left to right): Dick Stayberg, Ken Scherzer, Verlin Curtis, Doug Strain, Ed Swenson, Gordon Shockey, Jim Kirwan.

By 1968, Paul Lintner had returned to ESI from Mikros, taking up as marketing director. Here he and Doug Dickinson, ESI's Southeast District Manager, discuss strategy at the Region 3 IEEE/ISA show at Cocoa Beach Florida that same year, a show aimed specifically at industries serving the space program.

Who could "resist" what ESI was cooking up in 1968?

It was not for lack of trying that ESI had drifted into the doldrums. As far back as 1954 Doug and Clayton Strain, along with Rockwood and Morgan, had agreed to a budget goal of least 15% of annual sales for research and development. As the ESIAC and Mikros clearly indicated, they were good for their word. Doug, Rocky and Merle certainly had open minds, but finding new projects was not that easy. During the Sixties numerous ideas got funded, in hopes that one would strike pay dirt. An intuitive young engineer, Steve Supalla, came to Doug with an idea for a new motorcycle shock absorber. For months, prototypes came out of the shop and Supalla roared up and down the shoulder of Highway 26 testing each one. Shock absorbers failed to pan out, but there was no dearth of ideas. Strain himself came up with the "Ecco-Clean Washing Machine." Believing that hotels, motels, and especially hospitals, would love a machine that could do linens right in each room, rather than maintain a large linen inventory and laundry facilities, Strain got the idea for a machine that would use solvents for cleaning and a microwave to dry the linens. Cleaned and dried right in the room, they could be put right back on the bed and in the bathroom. Having tinkered with various prototypes, Strain approached a number of companies that manufactured washers and dryers, but without success.

One thing was certain, however, from the very earliest days of the company's existence, in tough times the ESI "family" faced trouble together. No layoffs occurred; rather, each employee opted to take fewer hours. One particularly vivid example of the company's willingness to consider creative solutions to cyclical downturns was the creation of ESI's subsidiary "Akros." Having rebuilt the company's manufacturing base after the fire, Rockwood and Strain had one of the most well-equipped and sophisticated machine shops in Oregon. This was the heyday of vertical integration in high technology, and ESI was right in step. The machine shop, the sheet metal shop, the paint shop, and the anodizing shop were all state-of-the-art operations that supported the design, manufacture and finishing of ESI's entire product line. For a time the company even had injection molding equipment. But when business fell off, these components of the business had little to do. So the Akros subsidiary represented a way to put ESI's excess shop capacity to use by taking outside bids. Rockwood, Hollis Smith, Don Smith, Erwin Zander and others recalled how well the Akros format worked. Akros did custom work for a variety of companies, from Sun Music to Tektronix. And during the doldrums of the late Sixties, Akros certainly was a blessing to the ESI family. Inevitably, however, it became a mixed blessing, since as business would pick up, Akros would be forced to cut its customers loose in order to return to the inside work at ESI. In the end, this made for bad relations with customers who had come to depend on Akros. Resuscitated briefly in the Seventies, Akros faded away, and by the Eighties ESI began to divest itself of its various shop operations. But by that time, layoffs had indeed come to Sunset Science Park. In the late Sixties, however, such creative flexibility stood the company in very good stead.

Not that ESI had forsaken its bread and butter – the precision instrument line – but by the late 1960's insiders knew that this was a market with an increasingly limited future. Merle Morgan saw the handwriting on the wall. And even a new employee, Larry Rapp, who arrived at ESI in 1966, could tell almost immediately that things would have to change:

> The first project I worked on when I came here, before we started the meter calibrator, was a quartz crystal capacitor. One of the people at the U.S.

Standards Lab had given Doug the idea. We polished pieces of quartz, hand polished them to about three inches in diameter. Then we sealed them in a stainless steel case, and then to be able to handle the temperature coefficient, we wound special resistors and embedded them in the case so we could measure the temperature and make the calculation for the capacitance. I think we built twenty-five of those. The world market, I think, was five. Doug wanted to build the most accurate capacitance standard ever built. In fact, the National Bureau of Standards in Washington, D.C., still uses one of them.

In retrospect, things are always so clear. Yet in 1968 and 1969, no such clarity seemed to exist. What was ESI's future? Where were new markets that would allow the company to grow? And how on earth would ESI fund its growth? No one in 1969 could yet know that within two years all of these questions would be answered decisively. Doug Strain's passion, indeed obsession, with precision; the experience with synchro motors on the ESIAC; the knowledge of electron micro devices from Mikros; the hard-earned marketing savvy of the ESIAC and Mikros teams; ESI's familiarity with trimming resistors to value; all of these would all combine in the hands of a few young turks – Ed Swenson, Tom Richardson, Don Cutler, Bob Pailthrop, George Vincent (a not- so-young turk) and Paul Lintner – to transform the company.

In 1969 the future lay just over the horizon.

AT THE RIGHT PLACE AT THE RIGHT TIME 1969-1974

By 1971 Laser Systems had arrived, and these were the men who sold them, gathered behind two key components of the Model 25 Laser Trimmer: on the left, the scanner module and on the right the standards drawer.

Seated (left to right): Ken Scherzer, Tom White, Doug Dickinson, Dwayne Erickson, Bill Lyon, Don Bell.

Standing (left to right): Doug Strain, Ed Swenson, Paul Lintner, Bill Greer, Stan Gressel, Jack Henderson.

Good Fortune in Failure

From the very earliest days, one of the consistent threads in the history of Electro-Measurements and ESI has been the company's eagerness to partner up with customers to insure that the instruments the company engineered met their customers' needs. Often, this meant that engineers assisted customers in installing their instruments, trained end users on site, and helped customers develop new applications for their instruments. This commitment to partnership with customers even led to the creation of an experimental laboratory at ESI specifically designed so that customers could come to ESI and participate in the development of new and customized systems. Such close support, before, during and after the sale has helped to set ESI off from many of its competitors, and in the 1950's and 1960's was particularly helpful in the many different government contracts awarded ESI, particularly with NASA and the U.S. Air Force.

It is ironic that the origins of ESI's greatest success should begin in failure, but that is precisely what happened. For years ESI had supplied the Air Force with "orange boxes," an array of standards instruments in a large orange metal housing that the Air Force could use on air bases to calibrate the more portable equipment used on the flight line in

the routine maintenance of aircraft. One of the instruments the Air Force used was a volt/amp meter, the Simpson 260VOM, an analog meter that could measure voltage, current, and resistance. The Air Force had tens of thousands of the Simpson meters in bases all over the world, and airmen found it inconvenient to bring each one to the "orange box" standards station on base for checks and re-calibration. So in 1966, working closely with the Air Force, ESI kicked off a project to engineer a meter calibrator, a portable instrument that an airman could take out on the flight line to check the Simpson meters. Of key importance to the meter calibrator project was the participation of a young engineer, Dick Schomburg, ESI's first digital engineer. Schomburg's work foreshadowed ESI's entry into digital electronics.

Plans called for the ESI meter calibrator to have a card reader, and to use IBM punch cards individually punched for different tests. The Simpson meter could be checked against the programmed values from the punch cards, and a teletype machine would print out the accuracy of the meter, its settings and where it needed re-calibration. Development and engineering of the ESI Model 70 meter calibrator took time, in fact too much time. During the almost three years of the project, John Fluke Company developed a digital volt meter. Within a very short time, the Fluke digital volt meter swept the market, thereby completely undercutting the ESI Model 70, which could not calibrate the digital volt meters that had so rapidly replaced the Simpson meters.

At $25,000, the Model 70 meter calibration system was ESI's most expensive single product when it appeared in 1969. And although the company sold only a handful, it served as the intellectual and engineering springboard for something much more promising. Since the mid-Sixties, parallel to the meter calibrator, the company had begun to think in terms of more complex instrument systems. ESI pioneered a new resistance measurement system that grouped as many as four smaller systems together – the Model 242DL resistance measuring system, two Model 123DL resistance comparison systems, and a Model 701DL capacitance measuring system – into a complete production testing system. Equally important, it had become clear that the digital world had indeed arrived. While Strain and Morgan openly mourned the demise of the analog world, others embraced a digital future. Among the earliest converts were a young new engineer, Don

Cutler, who came to ESI in 1968, and Ed Swenson, who as the chief applications engineer for the ESIAC had seen first-hand in the field how brutally digital computers had elbowed the analog computer aside.

Partnering Up

A native of Oregon, Ed Swenson was born in Portland in 1939 of Oregon pioneer stock. A graduate of Lincoln High School, in 1956 he enrolled at Pacific University, graduating in 1960 with a double major in physics and math. At Pacific, Swenson worked with Tom Holce, who was deep into his electron microscope project and teaching at the university. After a year at Oregon State University, during which he discovered that graduate mathematics was "probably not my cup of tea," Swenson returned to Portland in search of a job. Naturally, he contacted his old instructor and friend, Tom Holce, who by now was working with Paul Lintner in the Mikros subsidiary of ESI on their electron microscope project. Holce introduced Swenson to Lintner, who had recently been immersed in marketing the ESIAC and was now on the Mikros project. In late June of 1961, Ed Swenson began to work for ESI as an applications engineer on the ESIAC. With the end of the ESIAC, Swenson's focus shifted to resistance measurement systems. Swenson's engineering talents were matched, indeed exceeded, by his ability to work with customers in the field.

Among his most important customers was Western Electric, whose plant in Winston-Salem, North Carolina, made resistors and by 1969 had installed a number of ESI resistance measurement systems on their production line in the manufacture of telephone equipment and long-distance switching systems. And at this point things began to come together. The ESI resistance measurement systems favored by Western Electric were exquisitely precise, reflecting the influence of Doug Strain and his unwavering devotion to precision. But unlike other ESI analog products, the system also included digital electronics. Cutler, ESI's earliest and key laser systems engineer, whose engineering contributions over the years cannot be understated, and others on the project added scanners and other features that allowed the system to process unheard of numbers of resistors as they came down the line. Installed by Don Cutler and Larry Rapp, the entire system was computer-controlled, linked to a computer that Western Electric bought from Varian.

In the space of a few months, news traveled within Western Electric of how remarkably well ESI's new system worked in the Winston-Salem plant. At Western Electric's main laboratory in North Andover, Massachusetts, engineers were working on new ways to manufacture and "trim" resistors to value. Earlier, resistors consisting of copper wire coils were trimmed by cutting or sanding the outer surface of the coil, thinning the exposed wires and altering the resistance value of the coil. As the electronics industry matured, resistors were created by the application of a thin film of tantalum onto a base or substrate, often of ceramic material. Competition among electronics companies and their laboratories was fierce. Bell Labs and IBM had developed a process of trimming thin film resistors by focusing a needle-like blast of fine sand at the thin film resistor, abrading off material to bring the resistor to value. It was messy, imprecise, and Bell Labs' resistors had problems. So at North Andover, Western Electric wanted to go in a different direction: anodization.

ESI's Model SP 2820 Automatic Resistance Measuring System that Larry Rapp (left) and Don Cutler installed for Western Electric in Winston-Salem, North Carolina in 1969. Doug Strain is on the right.

Working closely together, Western Electric, Swenson, Cutler and their team at ESI helped to design the new process. "They put a gel on the top surface of the resistor," recalled Swenson, "and passed a current through it." This slowly changed the surface of the resistor into an oxide. "And you could do that in a precise way by passing pulses of current through it, and when it came to value, you shut it off. And so we built the bridges that they hooked up to their own anodization systems, ultimately we built the complete system for them." Not to be left out, Bell Labs joined in the project, making both Western Electric and Bell Labs the most advanced thin film resistor manufacturers, utilizing the anodization process based on ESI's bridge-based trimming systems. The key, thus far, had been the ability of Don Cutler and Bob Pailthorp to establish computer control functions to automate the system. A certain momentum began to build.

A Strange New Light

As ESI partnered with Western Electric and Bell Labs to create automated trimming systems for anodized thin film resistors, IBM still relied on "rock throwing," or sandblasting their resistors to value. Still, Ed Swenson began to look in a different direction. Even though they liked ESI's trimming systems, the folks at Bell Labs had the nagging feeling that there was something better. In a backwater corner of Bell Labs, a few people were building and experimenting with lasers. At the same time, there were several companies beginning to manufacture lasers by the late Sixties, namely: Colrad, Holobeam, Coherant Radiation and Quantronix. Simultaneously, Teradyne Applied Systems and Micronics began to manufacture systems, and were buying lasers from all four of these early producers. Micronics eventually began to produce their own YAG lasers. As Swenson made his customer visits throughout the electronics industry in 1968 and 1969, from time to time he would see a laser in a lab or in an experimental setting. In addition, first a trickle and gradually a stream of papers and articles began to appear at conferences and in journals about laser design and application.

"Laser," or light amplification by stimulated emission of radiation, was invented in 1960. Laser has become the term for the creation, amplification and transmission of a narrow, coherent beam of light. Unlike ordinary light that comprises an infinite variety of random wavelengths, the "coherent" light produced by a laser consists of light waves of the identical wavelength and perfectly coordinated, or "in phase" with one another. Such a focused beam, coherent and phased, offers a variety of uses, from highly accurate line-of-sight measurement and range-finding equipment to medical, industrial and military applications involving cutting and burning at a focused point. Lasers vary widely, depending upon the strength of the power supply, the material used for light emission, and the nature of the beam, whether steady or pulsed. Some lasers use gas or liquid as the light source, others a semiconductor diode. More often, however, the light emitted by a laser comes from a polished crystal that has been subjected to sufficient energy to excite atoms and molecules in the crystal. Many different crystals have been used; the first laser used a polished ruby rod, thus emitting a red beam. As the atoms or molecules become excited, they emit radiation in the form of photons. Photons of the same frequency and phase make up the coherent light beam produced by the laser.

Laser development in the Sixties was a highly experimental affair. Frequently, early

Sales Representative Bill Greer demos a prototype Model 16 Laser Trimmer with a CO_2 laser in 1970.

lasers used so much power, and became so hot, that they required elaborate cooling mechanisms, extensive plumbing and hundreds of gallons of water. As Ed Swenson became more and more intrigued with lasers, he took his ideas to Paul Lintner, who by 1969 was vice-president of marketing. With Lintner's encouragement, Swenson bought several lasers, installing them in a lab at ESI where Don Cutler, Tom Richardson, George Vincent, Bob Pailthorp, Larry Rapp and others could play with them. Bell Labs were making their own lasers, but the gang in the ESI lab thought the most interesting laser was that made by Holobeam, of Paramus New Jersey.

During 1969, as Swenson shuttled between Bell Labs, Western Electric, Holobeam, DuPont and ESI, Cutler, Richardson and company laid the groundwork for a series of experiments aimed at determining whether lasers could trim resistors, and if so, which kind of laser did it best. Initial results, in conjunction with Arvin Systems, resulted in several prototypes. Within a short time, Arvin Systems was out of the picture, and by late 1970, ESI had built its first laser trimmer, the Model 20. Throughout 1970 and early 1971 ESI's experiments continued. There were several problems: what type of laser was best, and exactly how the beam could be positioned for accurate trimming? Beam positioning was, and continues to be, one of the most difficult problems in the manufacture of laser trimming devices. Throughout the Seventies, Cutler, Pailthorp, Supalla and Ellsworth would work to perfect the mechanics of a beam-positioning system that combined an "X/Y table," the high-performance motors that would move the table under the laser beam. The beam, too, had to be positioned, as did the probes that descended onto the circuits held on the X/Y table. These challenges began in the planning stages of the Model 20, and would continue through succeeding Models 25 and 44.

Luckily, the choice of which laser to use was more easily settled: ultimately, ESI's engineers eliminated not only various crystals and diodes, but gas lasers as well. The CO_2 laser, for instance, whose wavelength made it suitable for high-powered cutting and scribing, was unsuited to the fine work of trimming resistors. Ultimately, in a paper that Swenson, Cutler, Vincent and Richardson presented in 1971 at the Conference on Hydrogen Manufacturing Technology, ESI made public its findings. The best laser for trimming thin film resistors was an yttrium aluminum garnet, or YAG, laser. A solid-state, one-micron laser, the YAG emitted a beam of almost infrared light, accurate enough for precision use.

It had been a painstaking development process, as Ed Swenson recalled:

> We figured out that the YAG was the laser of choice. George Vincent, Tom Richardson and I did work with DuPont, the major supplier of the materials used to build a resistor, and we did a study. Compared to how easy it is today, in those days it was just a painful, painful manual gathering of data, writing down readings, and then putting them in an oven and letting them age for a hundred hours, and then bringing them out and re-measuring them. But we didn't have the kinds of computerized automatic data-taking, data-logging instruments, so these studies were very, very difficult, since it was manual data-taking and tabulation, manipulating it with a hand calculator.... But they were watershed studies... and I think that [these studies] really defined that ESI was the company that understood the material and the laser and how to measure it. So we became The Guys – if you wanted to do precision stuff, you wanted to do good trimming, you came to ESI.

So all the pieces were in place: ESI's utter dedication to precision, a company value from the very beginning, emphasized countless times by Doug Strain as he pursued his

Don Cutler, standing, discussing an aspect of the Model 20, with (seated, left to right): Art Albin, Ed Swenson, Tom Richardson and Mike Ellsworth.

ESI's first commercially successful Laser Trimmer, the Model 20A, with the delighted threesome of (left to right): Mike Ellsworth, Tom Richardson and Art Albin.

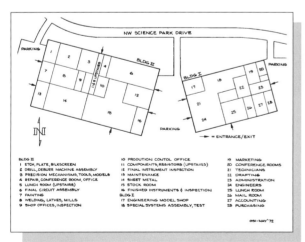

Propelled by the sales of the Model 20 Laser Trimmer, ESI embarked on an expansion in 1971-1972. Rocky Rockwood presided over the construction of Building II, adjacent to Building I, and the remaining shop and manufacturing operations from the Macadam plant moved to Science Park.

quest to place instruments in standards laboratories the world over; the hard-learned lessons that the electronics world had turned digital; a depth of experience with micro-mechanisms and automated systems from building automated resistance trimming systems for Western Electric; and, finally, a leading edge command of the infant laser technology. Ultimately, good luck comes from making your own breaks. By establishing its command of high-precision laser trimming, ESI defined its market, effectively guiding potential competitors away from the precision market – telephone filter networks, automotive circuits, television components – and into the passive resistor market.

With its line of anodization trimming systems already selling well to Western Electric, ESI found its first customer for the Model 20 laser trimmer: RCA. RCA wanted to revolutionize its television design and production. Hard hit by Japanese competition, and desperately trying to reduce labor costs, RCA conceived of a fully-automated plant that could make use of the most advanced chip circuit design. The idea was to condense the circuitry into thirteen chips, manufacture, test, assemble, and ship from the new plant in Indianapolis, Indiana. So in the summer of 1971, in a special area set aside in Building I, the one functioning Model 20 worked around the clock producing chips for RCA's initial order for 100 RCA XL100 Color TV sets. By the fall, ESI had not only produced chips for RCA, but enough laser trimming stations to get RCA up and running in the XL100 plant in Indianapolis.

The View from 1972

By 1972 ESI stood at the very edge of a new frontier, and the view was breathtaking. The company itself was in very capable hands. Doug Strain, president and chairman, was the intellectual and spiritual leader of the company. By the early Seventies, Doug displayed a dizzying array of interests, from the International Standards Association on the one hand, to local charitable and educational issues on the other. Clayton Strain had retired in 1968, and Charlie Davis now managed ESI on a day-to-day basis as secretary-treasurer, the *de facto* chief operating officer. Rockwood's organizational and manufacturing skills, so evident in the construction of ESI's new buildings and in the finely-tuned manufacturing operations of the company, complemented Davis' fiscal and operational gifts. The least visible of the "Four Horsemen," since the ESIAC, Merle Morgan contented himself with a variety of projects in his laboratory. Paul Lintner's marketing skill and vision meshed smoothly with the engineering drive of ESI's laser-driven young turks. Indeed, it was Lintner, who had the confidence of both Doug Strain and Ed Swenson, and it was Lintner who bridged the gap between the two. Attuned to the emerging semiconductor market, and evangelical in his belief in the future of the laser, the young Swenson seemed an irresistible force. On occasion, however, Swenson's irresistible force met his president's resistance. Strain's heart was in the standards lab and the instruments business, and by his own admission he was a reluctant convert to ESI's laser business. By 1972, however, ESI's laser had a momentum all its own, a momentum that had a way of overpowering whatever initial misgivings had existed.

In May 1972, at an employee banquet at the Multnomah Athletic Club, Doug Strain sang the praises of ESI's 200 employees, saluting the company's new business, and offering up a vision for a technologically advanced future, much of which became a reality a quarter of a century later:

By 1973 the Model 25 Resistance Trimming Laser System hit the market, occupying the pride of place at the International Society of Hybrid Manufacturers (ISHM) show in San Francisco that year.

...Without question, in my mind, the move to the age of communication is the wave of the future for many significant reasons. Fortunately, ESI has moved right into the middle of it in the past two years with investment of money and talent in the development of systems for the low-cost, high volume production of integrated circuit components. From the RCA XL100 Color TV chips that we trimmed in our plant last summer on our prototype laser trimming system to the anodization systems we delivered to Western Electric–Andover in the past year, we have moved into the heartland of the coming age of communication. Since our systems have gotten on stream, RCA has been able to make television sets competitively in Indianapolis instead of importing them from Japan, the costs have come tumbling down on long distance calls since the new Western Electric long lines transmission sets have been produced in increasing quantities and substantially reduced costs — thanks to ESI anodization sets, laser trimmers and scribers. Of course, it is not only RCA and Western Electric that are involved. ESI has also delivered such systems to Motorola, Honeywell, General Electric, DuPont, Dale Electronics, Lambda, Airco Speer Research and Tektronix in this country and to Garrett in Canada, Bosch in Germany, Siemens and Magneti-Marelli in Italy, Lucas Aerospace in England — to name only a few. And this is only the beginning. The Federal dataways are not yet in place, picturephone needs many billions of dollars invested in equipment to put in each of our homes, many satellites are yet to be put in place and we still have not adjusted our life style to a way of living that is more dependent upon communication than upon transportation. Between now and the turn of the century, these developments will have a great impact upon learning without classrooms, shopping without supermarkets, working without going to the factory, voting without polling places, national conventions without convention halls and cosmopolitan living without cities.

"Distance learning," "internet shopping," "telecommuting," "vote by mail," "national electronic town meetings," and "the world wide web" did not exist in 1972, but Doug Strain imagined them. He, and others at ESI, knew that they would have a hand in almost all of them.

The take-off of laser trimming systems in the early 1970's required frequent strategy sessions, such as the one here involving (left to right): Tom Richardson, Charlie Davis, Doug Strain, Paul Lintner and Merle Morgan.

In his remarks at the Multnomah Athletic Club, Strain had offered an abbreviated list of the company's customers. It was only 1972. What he and his audience well knew, was that ESI was already engineering the next generation laser trimmer, the Model 25. The Model 25 Resistance Trimming Laser System came out in 1973 to unanimous acclaim. It was faster, incorporating increased automation. Many of ESI's oldest and best customers now clamored for the newest systems: Bendix, Boeing, Grumman Aircraft Company, Hughes Aircraft Company, IBM, Litton Industries, Lockheed, McDonnell-Douglas, Martin-Marietta, NASA, Philco-Ford, Raytheon, Sperry Rand-Univac, Union Carbide, U.S. Department of Defense, and Westinghouse rounded out just the top tier. ESI was represented by sales representatives on every continent save Antarctica. Sales of the Model 25 in Western Europe penetrated every market, even France, whose political and economic nationalism made French companies exceedingly difficult customers to win over.

THE ROAD TO THE PUBLIC OFFERING 1974–1983

Wednesday, October 19, 1983, ESI goes public at $15 per share.

No Rest for the Successful

No sooner had the Model 25 made its debut than work began on yet a more sophisticated laser trimming system. To keep pace with its customers, and with the evident trend in the electronics industry toward thick film resistors, ESI engineers team had to design their new generation laser for thick film. The Model 44 Laser Trimming System took shape and the ESI laser team widened to include others, such as Dick Harris and Steve Supalla. ESI's best Model 25 customers, customers with multiple trimming systems, such as Western Electric, Automatic Electric, and a division of GE, Lenkirk Electric, were increasingly committed to thick film resistors: multiple layers of oxide and ion-infused dopant laid down on various substrate materials, from ceramic to silicon, to form the resistors, capacitors and gates of complex electronic circuitry. The Model 44 would use the same YAG laser and the same beam-positioning technology as the Model 25, but with a different operating system. In Don Cutler's words, the Model 44 came "with a lower cost, and a little more versatile instrument package on it that was a little simpler to use."

The development of the Model 44 Laser Trimming System, however, was not without its controversies. In a confrontation that would repeat itself over the years, ESI's devotion to precision clashed with the blunt realities of the market. The precision of thin film resistors appealed to Doug Strain. The advent of thick film, offering ease of manufacture and versatility of application, came at the sacrifice of the precision so dear to Strain's heart, and it took Cutler, Richardson, Swenson and their team some time to win their president over. Once again, Paul Lintner helped to guide the debate in a productive direction. Indeed, by 1976, when the Model 44 appeared, ESI's advertising campaign could ask:

> What do leading thick film and hybrid circuit manufacturers look for when it's time to pick a laser trimming system? Over 500 ESI systems installed worldwide show it's a "total system solution."

A winning combination: Paul Lintner, Doug Strain and the Model 44 Laser Trimming System.

In 1975, when Charlie Davis became the
Oregon Public Utilities Commissioner, ESI hired
Barton Alexander to replace Davis. Alexander,
shown here standing on the right, with Rocky
and Doug, served as Secretary/Treasurer.

- Proven performance
- Circuit throughput
- Cost competitive
- Dependable operation
- Technological leadership
- Turnkey software
- System versatility
- Worldwide sales and service
- Customer training
- Applications research and consultation

As troubled as he may have been with his engineers' insistence on the Model 44's
emphasis on thick film, Strain could hardly argue with the company's business success.
Well before the appearance of the Model 44, ESI's financial performance had been nothing short of phenomenal. In the decade between 1965 and 1974, net earnings had risen
508% from $65,282 to $331,339. In the same decade, earnings per share rose almost as
impressively, from $0.22 per share to $1.06 per share. In FY1976, the year the Model 44
made its debut, ESI shipped twenty laser trimmer units. From there the laser trimmer
rocket took off:

> Fiscal Year 1977: 37 units
> Fiscal Year 1978: 60 units
> Fiscal Year 1979: 92 units
> Fiscal Year 1980: 143 units

In five years, ESI's laser trimmer business had grown more than 700%. But not without
competition.

ESI's chief competitor was Teradyne, whose laser trimmers were cheaper, and less
accurate, but still attractive to customers willing to sacrifice precision for price. If it was
quality the customer wanted, however, ESI was the only choice. In the spring of 1978
the International Society for Hybrid Microelectronics met in Baltimore. In an effort to
impress those passing its booth at the show, Teradyne offered to inscribe the top surface
of a metal ruler with the name of the passerby, using their newest laser. One of those
who dropped by Teradyne's booth was ESI sales representative Doug Dickinson. Seeing
the job that Teradyne had done for Dickinson, Dick Harris took Dickson's ruler, stood it
on edge, and using ESI's Model 44 inscribed the ruler's thin edge, "Laser Scribed for
Douglas Dickinson By E.S.I.," in finely done letters roughly one-fifth the size of
Teradyne's.

Taking Stock

The spectacular growth of the company now cast the spotlight directly on a cluster
of questions: just who owned the company, who should be able to own stock, and how
could a true value be placed on the company? Since buying out his initial partners in
1953, Doug Strain had been the company's majority shareholder, a status that continued
even after Rockwood and Morgan joined Electro-Measurements with equity positions,
along with that of Clayton Strain. In 1954, with the creation of the employees' profit shar-

ing trust, the shareholders in effect agreed to limit their personal gain, although employees did not immediately receive equity interest in the company. During the Sixties, however, the ESI board began to grant options to a small number of key employees, and in January 1976 the board approved a resolution to issue stock to ESI employees through a stock purchase program. The details would take several years, but by 1979 ESI had restructured the profit sharing trust, the employee retirement trust and added an employee stock ownership plan, so that a portion of each employee's profit share could be used to purchase company stock.

Placing a value on the company had always been up to the board. The last time the ESI board had calculated a share price, in 1973, it was $9.25 per share. As the question of employee stock purchase surfaced, however, ESI looked outside for an impartial valuation of the company. In 1976, ESI turned to Kirk Knight & Co., Inc., of Menlo Park, California, for assistance in placing a value on ESI stock. Kirk Knight & Co. calculated a $3.8 million value on the company, and a fully diluted (i.e., after options were exercised, options that would be at lower prices than present value) value of $11.44 on each share of ESI stock. According to Kirk Knight the fully diluted share value of ESI stock rose during the coming years as steadily as did the sales of laser trimmers:

1977	$21.08
1978	$34.73
1979	$57.67

In 1980, ESI switched to a local company, Willamette Management Associates for its outside diluted share value calculation. Willamette Management's evaluation, as Kirk Knight's before it, was annualized according to the calendar year, and reflected the dramatic growth in sales and profitability at ESI by the end of the Seventies:

1980	$106.50
1981	$124.00

Doug Strain could bring a smile to anyone's face, and his sense of humor was renown throughout ESI. Here, in 1978, "Mom Strain" pitches the "MOM" program, the company's new computer-aided Management Resources Planning (MRP) system.

By 1982, the question of the value of the company, and of ESI's share value would take on greater urgency.

The breathtaking growth in sales between 1975 and 1981, the addition of new employees and more space, and the details of a more complex profit sharing formula that now included an employee stock purchase option, all posed great challenges. These were made more complicated by the fact that in March of 1975 Charlie Davis had resigned as secretary-treasurer to take an appointment as State Utilities Commissioner in Salem. Paul Lintner stepped in to fill in for Davis while the board began to search for a permanent replacement for Davis. By the fall of 1975, ESI had a new secretary/treasurer, L. Barton Alexander. A Harvard Business School graduate, Alexander came to ESI at a crucial time. Without doubt, he was instrumental in helping to streamline and update many administrative functions within ESI. His hand can be seen in the details of both an increased company pre-tax contribution to the Retirement Trust, as well as the Profit Sharing Stock Purchase Option Plan, in the overhaul of computer services from IBM to DEC, and in the details of expansion into two adjacent buildings to the west, designated Buildings III and IV.

Heinrich Stenger, whose marketing wizardry in ESI's Munich office, had by 1977 spurred his boss, Paul Lintner, to open a German marketing subsidiary, "ESI GmbH."

Paul Lintner

Freed from his additional duties as secretary/treasurer by Bart Alexander's arrival, Paul Lintner was able to concentrate on marketing and sales. It was not enough that by the mid-Seventies ESI built the world's best laser trimming systems, the company also had to market them, and here Paul Lintner's contribution was essential. Paul D. Lintner was born in Milan, Missouri, on June 12, 1932. Raised in Missouri and New Mexico, Lintner earned a BS in electrical engineering from UCLA. Prior to coming to ESI in 1959, Paul had worked as an engineer, first for the White Sands Proving Ground, and then for Shell Oil Company in Los Angeles. His rural childhood and his formative years in the West lent Paul Lintner a relaxed air. Those who knew him liked him; and those who worked with him came to respect his calm, his willingness to listen, and his ability to motivate those around him. People could see Paul's demonstrated ability "to manage every side of an issue" as he simultaneously won the trust of Ed Swenson and Doug Strain. He could see where Ed's grand and sometimes "wild" vision could take the company, and he could translate that vision into sales, growth and profitability that won Doug over.

Paul Lintner's gift was not only in guiding domestic growth for ESI, but in grasping clearly the potential for overseas growth as well. By the end of 1976, he had a well-oiled sales organization based in Germany, and had negotiated with Phillips N.V. in Holland to collaborate on opening a service center in Eindhoven, The Netherlands. By August 1977, under Lintner's direction, ESI opened a subsidiary in Germany, based in Munich, ESI, GmbH:

> ... facilities in Germany under the direct authority of the ESI Marketing Department would better serve our purpose there and in surrounding territory by providing better and faster service for customers and increased sales potential, all at lower cost than required to maintain the foreign representative relationship. The initial costs in establishing the location may be substantial, but net results should more than adequately support this decision.

To head the Munich office, ESI tapped its dynamic and very successful German representative, Heinrich Stenger. Within a year Lintner could report to the board that ESI GmbH had contributed ten percent of all orders, and produced an equally impressive ten percent return on investment.

In 1977, for the first time ESI had orders of over $10 million a year. The growth in sales, gross margins in excess of fifty percent and net profits between eight and twelve percent per year in the latter Seventies all put tremendous pressure on ESI's administration. In 1978, ESI's 84,000 square feet housed 340 employees and by 1980, these had grown to 171,000 square feet and 619 employees. Watching his company blossom, Doug Strain attempted to anticipate change by grooming Paul Lintner as his successor as president and chief operating officer, and in 1978 Strain tapped Lintner to lead ESI. Strain's wide spectrum of outside interests, plus his desire to reinvigorate the instrument line, all contributed to his decision, a move, however, that caught Bart Alexander off guard. By the summer of 1979, Alexander moved on to other opportunities.

As years went, 1979 was a pivotal year. So rapidly was ESI expanding that Rockwood, who initially requested $1 million in February from the board for new construction, came back in May with a request to increase : to $2.5 million. Within two more months the company would move to augment its building program with the purchase of the Sunset Valley School. A soon-to-be-vacant elementary school to the east of Sunset Science Park, ESI purchased the property with the assistance of Port of Portland Industrial Investment Bonds for $2.1 million. With an additional $500,000 of remodeling, the school was added to ESI's inventory as Building IX, and was occupied in 1980 by administration, finance, marketing and central computing.

Ambitions ran high in 1979, and for good reason. Success in Germany fueled ESI's initiative to break with its French representative, Tranchant, and set up its own subsidiary in France, SARL, headed by Olivier Dancer. Although the details of ESI SARL took several years to complete, the business plan for 1979-1980 took full notice of ESI s foreign success. In Paul Lintner's words: "Markets: we want ESI's computer controlled laser trimmers to maintain their market position: thick film – 50%; thin film – 90%." Indeed, looking to the Far East, ESI should anticipate a Japanese venture soon. As Lintner began to hit his stride, he proposed a new position, Vice President–Systems, to be filled by Ed Swenson. At the same time, Lintner, and board chairman Strain pushed for the addition of outside members on the board of directors, an idea that met with complete agreement among board members. Thus, at its November 1, 1979 meeting, the ESI Board of Directors welcomed its first two outside directors: William H. Kinsey, legal counsel to ESI, and William Walker, Vice President at Tektronix, and long-time friend of ESI. At the same meeting, the board also welcomed Bart Alexander's successor, O. Dean Finley, to the postition of comptroller.

In October 1978, ESI celebrated its 25th Anniversary, thereby contributing to the confusion as to the company's age. Although in 1978 it was calculated from 1953, when Doug Strain bought out his partners, the company was actually 34 years old dating to 1944 and Brown Engineering.

A Tale of Two Companies

For the next three years, events at ESI seemed to move in their own time/space continuum. On the one hand, the public could see the rapid and inexorable physical expansion of the company, as it grew to encompass nine buildings in and around the Sunset Science Park campus. In addition, the public witnessed a dazzling parade of engineering marvels issuing from the portals of ESI.

During the Seventies, scientists at various laboratories throughout the country experimented with conductive and resistive materials, seeking cheaper, lighter, faster media. While ceramic substrate material continued to dominate certain applications, particularly resistors, scientists increasingly gravitated to silicon. Silicon was cheap, lightweight, capable of housing a vast array of circuit architecture. Bell Labs led in silicon research by the late Seventies, which meant that ESI was also at the leading edge of silicon research, given the close partnership enjoyed by the two for over a decade. In fact, ESI had a special experimental lab just for Bell Labs engineers, who came out with the new circuits on silicon substrates to test their ideas with ESI's latest lasers. Swenson and his band were in such close contact with Bell Labs that they knew their job was to develop a new generation of pulsing lasers to meet Bell Labs' demands. What Bell Labs had in mind was to design circuits on silicon substrate that had multiple redundant pathways, so that when one circuit did not test out, it could be closed off, and another opened in its place.

The idea of "redundant circuits" was a brilliant breakthrough that to a significant degree reflected a deep cultural war between American semiconductor development and

In 1979, Doug Strain and Paul Lintner congratulate their comrades in arms as ESI hit a new high: over $20 million in systems and instruments shipped.

that of its chief competitor: Japan. The underlying problem faced by the semiconductor industry both here and abroad was one of yield. So minute, so delicate and so sensitive are the circuits laid down by the photo-resist screening of dopant onto a substrate, that in any given run upwards of eighty percent of the circuits might not function. The Japanese, who had been very quick to seize upon integrated circuits, miniaturization and semiconductors, believed that yield was a function of quality control and in particular "clean room" environments. Their clean rooms, the Japanese claimed, were far superior to American facilities. Consequently, Japanese electronics firms viewed redundancy as something of a sad American effort to make good circuits out of bad. Bell Labs and ESI, however, looked at it quite differently.

There were two questions. What if, on a silicon chip, redundant circuits could be engineered in at the outset? And when a circuit on a chip did not work, what if it could be "repaired" by means of a short pulse from a laser beam that would seal off the problem and another pulse that would open up a new circuit? If this could in fact be done, then yield could be radically improved. During 1978 and 1979 this is exactly what Bell Labs and ESI worked on, Bell Labs providing the silicon chips, ESI the experimental lasers. Then, as Ed Swenson recalled:

> In September 1979, at the International Solid-State Circuits Conference, Bell Labs gave just an absolutely marvelous paper — they'd actually done this in 8mm movie format — in which they showed pictures of a length [of silicon] being cut with the laser, and then they showed their inspection team looking at the crater [made by the laser in the silicon material]. And then they showed a pack train going down into the Grand Canyon to inspect it. It was just marvelously humorous, but it just absolutely set the conference on its ear. Everybody was just as excited as hell.

In 1980, ESI introduced its Model 80 MicroLase Laser Processing System, the first memory repair system.

With dizzying swiftness between 1980 and 1982, ESI extended its reach. Already in 1979, ESI had entered into a research partnership with the Texas Engineering Experiment Station, a high tech research institute created by Texas A&M University with the support of Texas Instruments. The relationship with Texas A&M would prove fruitful for ESI, since A&M, and now ESI, could draw on present and former Texas Instruments talent for research on future laser applications.

A measure of ESI's commitment to research and development can be seen in the budget proposed for fiscal year 1981 for "Innovation Projects." Dated July 17, 1980, the eleven-point proposal totaled $201,600:

1. YAG and Related Crystal Growing Projects
2. Optics Manufacturing
3. Model 44 and Model 80 Applications
4. Gallium Arsenide – Laser Interaction
5. Technical Seminars
6. Market Research of Future Industry Trends
7. CAD/CAM Investigation
8. Circuit Manufacturing Techniques
9. Innovative Electro Mechanical Design
10. Affiliations with Outside Institutions
11. Conferences, Seminars, Student Support

By 1981 ESI produced its own proprietary laser, thus freeing the company from its dependence on outside sources for its lasers. The same year, Lintner and company announced the creation of a sales and service subsidiary in Japan, ESI KK, in Tokyo. By 1982, the French subsidiary, ESI SARL, finally opened in Paris, and later that same year ESI Ltd. opened in London.

If the negotiations for opening a subsidiary in France were protracted and vexing, this was as much due to the vicissitudes of the French legal system as to the tenacious delaying tactics of Tranchant. But the time and energy it took to establish a beachhead in Japan dwarfed even ESI's efforts in France. By 1982 the Japanese electronics industry was, in business and financial terms, virtually a nation unto itself. With labor costs a fraction of those in the U.S., with vertical integration that often included their own banks, and with government cooperation in every aspect of their competition with foreign enterprises, Japanese electronics companies enjoyed the luxury of looking down on all but the largest and most successful American electronics companies. For years ESI had hit a bamboo wall trying to introduce memory repair in Japan. Nikon dominated the laser in Japan. Now, with the advent of the Model 80 MicroLase system, ESI hoped the reception would be different. Alas, as Swenson recalled, the Japanese simply wrote off the Model 80 as an embarrassing attempt to make good circuits out of bad.

In the late summer of 1982, Swenson and ESI's Japanese representatives had toured virtually all of the leading Japanese electronics manufacturers: NEC, Hitachi, Sony, Matsushita, the works. Everywhere they went they met with polite but firm rejections. The travelling was exhausting: it was hot; the trains and subways were choked with people; and the language barrier was wearing Ed down. The last stop, the very last stop, was Toshiba, on the outskirts of Tokyo. The meeting began. And the same thing that had always happened began again: Ed would say ten words, the representative translating would say fifty; Ed would say twenty, the rep would say a hundred. "I just couldn't tell what he was telling them, and I wasn't sure the message was getting across." Ed figited. "I'm sure I must've looked tired, and, you know discouraged after three weeks of hearing 'No.'" And then something wonderful happened:

One of the group, Dr. Koryama, looked up and said, "Swenson-San, wouldn't this be a hell of a lot easier in English?" And I looked at him with my face red, and so he said, "Let me introduce myself." And then he went around introducing each of the guys around the table, all about the same age as he, all with PhD's from American universities. He was a University of Minnesota PhD, and the next one was from Cal Tech, the next from Berkeley, the next from Stanford.

These were all heavy-hitters, all U.S.-educated, all young, all with specific specialties around semiconductor processes. And we took off....

The Toshiba team had already gone down the road to address redundancy, but in the direction of fuses, so that when Swenson began to describe redundant circuitry and laser memory repair, they became more and more excited. Ultimately Toshiba bought a Model 80 to experiment with, and within several months had ordered more. ESI had its beachhead. Soon, scrambling to catch up with Toshiba, other Japanese companies came calling on ESI.

A Business Unit, a Calcumeter, and a Subsidiary

The breadth of the company's reach had grown to include first Germany, and now Japan, France and Great Britain, and in 1982 extended for the first time to the acquisition of another company. While much of the high-flying success of ESI by the late Seventies and early Eighties seemed to rest on the development of laser systems, the continued success of the company's bedrock instrument line should not be overlooked. The decade of the 1970's saw the transformation of the instrument line to digital format with the introduction of the Model 1700 Digital Ohmmeter in 1973. In addition, as ESI became more and more familiar with both systems and microprocessors, the instrument line kept pace. In 1977, the Model 296 and the Model 410 Series automatic impedance meters ushered ESI into high-speed production with microprocessor control. By 1980, the instrument line included the very newest video display technology, with the release of the Model 2100 VideoBridge.

The future of ESI's instrument business was a matter dear to the hearts of many of the company's oldest employees. Even as he consciously scaled back his administrative duties, Doug Strain continued to devote considerable creative energy to the instrument line. In no small measure due to his influence, ESI created a Portable Instrument Business Unit in 1978, technically a wholly-owned subsidiary called Micrometrics. At the core of his initiative was Strain's desire to enter into the hand-held instrument market. By applying the same microchip technology that powered pocket calculators, Strain sought to engineer a hand-held multimeter, a multi-function field instrument. He called it the Calcumeter, and when it appeared in 1978, it got rave reviews, such as the one in *Electronic Design:*

> Picture a processing digital multimeter that memorizes, averages, sorts, calculates, bleeps warnings and communicates with other instruments or devices. Sound like a typical DDM? It isn't. It's the Calcumeter 4100 – the first hand-held meter than can do all those things.
>
> Developed by Electro Scientific Industries, the 4100 is a DVM chip blended with a CMOS calculator type µP chip set. However, the 4100 goes beyond a simple marriage of an autoranging 3-1/2-digit meter to a calculator: It processes measured data to convert the raw input signal into a desired engineering result.

"The model 410 features a load of bells and whistles, so we photographed it in the appropriate setting for our introductory advertisement," read the caption in **The ESI Bridge**. In the end, the ad seemed to attract more attention in Europe than at home, hardly heralding the dawn of a new day in instrument ads.

Special function keys promise a measuring power that could save you hours of design time a week. The calculator input can come from measurements, user input via the keyboard, or – most importantly – from both. And the bidirectional serial data port brings a new dimension to "single handed" field or bench measurement.

With all its systems look-alike features, the Calcumeter sports an eyebrow-lifting price tag of $389 – a far cry from the $3000 and up you'll pay for systems units.

The Calcumeter seemed like a home run. Even if you bought every single accessory, from printer to temperature probe, from carrying case to owner's handbook, the entire setup would cost $910.00, plus $3.50 shipping and handling. Sadly, rather than a home run, the Calcumeter was just a deep fly ball. While the Calcumeter engineering team worked to design an instrument that would live up to ESI's demanding precision standards and integrate the versatility of its many features, the competition went in two different directions. At John Fluke and at Hewlett-Packard, where precision was not the same issue for hand-held field instruments, both companies came out with rugged, less accurate instruments whose lower price undercut the Calcumeter's market. In Japan, on the other hand, several companies quickly followed suit, producing instruments almost identical to the Calcumeter at one-third the price. As the result, to be competitive, the price of the Calcumeter fell below cost. "It was as if we put a $100 bill in every Calcumeter box we shipped," recalled Charlie Davis, who by late 1979 had returned from Salem and resumed his duties as secretary/treasurer.

But as with other projects that had not fully panned out, the Calcumeter project had beneficial by-products. First, it breathed new life into the instrument business. Clearly, ESI intended to be a player in the microprocessor instrument business, and this boded well. One of the people heavily involved with the Calcumeter project was Jim Currier. And it was Currier, with the active support of Paul Lintner, who now sought new opportunities linked to the instrument line. One customer, a company in Escondido, California, was particularly interesting to Currier and Lintner: Palomar Systems and Machines. Founded in 1979, Palomar was a manufacturer of high speed machine systems for the automated handling and processing of small parts, particularly for the chip component manufacturing industry. ESI and Palomar began to work closely to integrate their systems, making use of ESI's automated test systems and Palomar's automated handling systems to build fully integrated, automated chip capacitor test lines. By 1981 ESI and Palomar were working so closely together that in January 1982 they announced the joint development of the Model 11 Chip Capacitor Test System, at the center of which was ESI's Model 296 LRC Meter, as well as ESI scanners and motor controls. The Palomar Model 11 was used for testing the capacitance and dissipation factor of multi-layer ceramic chip capacitors. The system boosted productivity eight-fold over existing systems, to a throughput rate exceeding 40,000 parts per hour. The first in the Model 11's long line of enthusiastic customers were AVX, Union Carbide and Corning.

To Currier and Lintner, a match between ESI and Palomar seemed like a natural. The owners of Palomar, Denver Braden, Keith Brown and Dick Moore seemed to agree, and in the same month, January 1982, the two companies announced that ESI would acquire Palomar as a wholly-owned subsidiary of ESI. The six Palomar shareholders received ESI shares in exchange for their Palomar equity holdings. In their joint

Whether offered in giant size or as an appetizer, the Calcumeter just never found a market. Despite Doug's confidence, ESI's sales force had a tough job with the Calcumeter, even if it was frosted, as it was at its European roll-out in Amsterdam, where (left to right) Tim Krouse, Jim Currier and Dick Donica served up Calcumeter petits fours.

In February 1982, ESI acquired Palomar Systems, of
Escondido, California. The acquisition was the fruit of
Jim Currier's work with Palomar, one of ESI's customers,
and represented the first in a long series of acquisitions
by ESI. Present at the formal agreement were: (seated
from left) Paul Lintner and Palomar's Dick Moore,
(standing from the left) Keith Brown of Palomar, Dean
Finley, Palomar's Denver Braden, and Jim Currier.

announcement, ESI and Palomar stated that "their marriage will benefit the industry,
since it provides ESI with the capability of offering customers complete handling/testing
systems from a single source."

A Question of Money

The details of the ESI-Palomar deal were worked out by a small underwriting
house, Eberstadt Investment Company. ESI had been working with Eberstadt for some
time, and the Palomar deal threw into stark relief two interrelated problems that had
bedeviled the company for years: working capital and share price. These were issues
known to the board and to ESI's senior management team, but to few others. Since the
mid-1970's ESI had received annual third-party assessments of company value and share
price, but this was only of limited value. ESI shares were internal. There was no market
in ESI shares, and hence the financial value of shares to the company was quite limited,
for the company could not sell shares to raise capital. Thus, ESI was dependent upon the
largesse of the U.S. Bank.

With the arrival of Dean Finley, who succeeded Bart Alexander, senior management
heard a new voice address the company's financial predicament. In January 1980, Finley
issued the first of what became his trademark quarterly reports to the board. In this first
report he sounded a warning. The rapid expansion of ESI during the late Seventies had
dramatically increased the assets of the company, over $6 million in the last six months
alone, $12.8 million in the past eighteen months. But this growth in assets – basically
plant and equipment – was running at nearly four times the rate of growth of net
income. "Since there have been very few equity additions to the company, the difference
– approximately $9 million – is called debt," Finley cautioned. Because ESI had bor-
rowed to finance its growth, and since interest rates were high, debt service alone was
$950,000 per year, and growing:

> Using an operating income rate of 23% of sales (the current rate) this
> means that sales of over $4 million are needed just to pay interest on borrowed
> funds. Another way to view this financial position is to compare equity/debt
> ratios. At May 31, 1978, ESI had $1.11 of equity for each $1.00 in liabilities; at
> November 30, 1979, this ratio was $0.56 for each $1.00 in liabilities – a signifi-
> cant change in a relatively short time period… So long as the company remains
> very profitable there are advantages to borrowing funds to finance growth,
> even at current high interest rates. The downside risk is greater, however, and
> the company must be prepared to react quickly to changes in conditions.

Dean Finley came to ESI from Pacific University, where he had been Vice-President
of Finance. Born in Nebraska in 1929, Finley was eleven when his family moved to
Southern California in 1940. Graduating from high school in 1947, Finley briefly attended
college before he joined the Navy in 1948, qualifying for Naval Flight School. From 1951
to 1954 he served as a carrier pilot. After his tour he resumed his studies, graduating
from UCLA in 1959 in Accounting. For the next four years he worked for Arthur
Andersen & Company. In 1963 he went to work for a start-up electronics firm in Orange
County, Dana Laboratories, a new venture started by four former Beckman Instruments
men. By 1976, Finley was ready for a change, and applied for the ESI position that was
eventually filled by Bart Alexander. But he had made a deep impression on Doug Strain,

who was at the time early in his long and illustrious tenure as a Trustee at Pacific University. Pacific needed a financial officer, Doug had just the man, and from 1976 to 1979, Finley worked at Pacific.

Perhaps it was their similar high school experiences in Southern California, perhaps his experience with Dana Laboratories, but Dean Finley had something that Doug liked. Quiet, gentle, always positive, a team player and a straight-shooter, Finley fit perfectly with Doug's value system and ESI's culture. "I think people immediately thought Dean was another Paul Lintner/Doug Strain type person," recalled Larry Rapp, who worked closely with Finley, "very similar personalities, easy-going, you know, got along with all the people in the building."

The immediate relief at Dean Finley's arrival was evident throughout the company. But his warning about the financial clouds on ESI's horizon went unnoticed. Within senior management, the voices of Rockwood and Swenson called for increased spending, the former on facilities and manufacturing, the latter on engineering. By April 1980, Finley's next quarterly report pleaded further caution, as operating expenses now exceeded the forecasted number by $200,000: "the task for 1981 is clearly going to be to control expenses; preserve profit margins. If this is not accomplished, increased working capital requirements will absorb net income and very little funding for capital expansion will be available." The very next day the board approved a new borrowing resolution with U.S. Bank, even as Finley's words rang in their ears, "that the large commitments for expansion and capital equipment were usurping the financial strength of the company." Within a month the board would pass yet another corporate resolution to increase ESI's borrowing to $12 million.

Later that summer, in August 1980, as one by one members of Lintner's management team reported bullish sales projections to the board, Finley again tried to get their attention. This year, he pointed out, debt service alone stood at $1.05 million, and in the coming year would grow to $1.2 million, requiring $8 million in sales just to pay interest on ESI's loan balance in fiscal 1981. Even as he spoke, sales had begun to fall off. But building, and tooling up for the bullish forecasts continued. The board minutes of January 1981 reflect this air of unreality: "Board discussion focused on the possibility that the growth expectations were too low...." And by April U.S. Bank had agreed to loan ESI another $10 million at 15%, even as Finley reported that sales and income had continued to drop in the third quarter. "People and facilities" had continued to grow in fiscal 1981, the former from 467 to 617, the latter by 66%. "These two increases," cautioned Finley, "coupled with essentially level sales dollars, can only translate to decreased earnings." Efforts to finesse the problem with Christmas closures and shorter weeks in January had not worked: "They cannot be expected to cancel out the higher personnel and facilities costs." Something had to be done.

Finally, Dean Finley's message seemed to have registered. At the July board meeting, Paul Lintner, who was about to elevate Finley to Vice President for Finance, joined him to re-enforce the need for concern over ESI's position:

> For the second successive year the balance sheet shows an increase in fixed assets which exceeds the sum of depreciation and net income. Currently, 41% of our total assets are in non-current categories, and this trend toward increases in fixed assets places us in a non-flexible position which creates a heavy financial load to carry.

Dean Finley, whose low-key style suited the Paul Lintner era perfectly.

How a deal is put together. In Frankfurt, West Germany, in 1971, Bill Greer (lower right) puts the finishing touches on negotiations for a major laser trimmer purchase with executives from the German electronics firm of Bosch.

By the early 1980's, ESI's success was written not only on its bottom line, but painted on its walls. The "campus" now sprawled to include almost a dozen buildings, as maintenance staff scrambled to remodel, renovate and refurbish. Dallas Buchman (top), shown here in a characteristic shot, has probably painted every square inch of ESI's interior at one time or another over the past twenty-five years. No amount of interior decoration, however, could completely make over Building IX (center), the former school ESI remodeled in the early 1980's for its headquarters building. Not even exterior camouflage (bottom) could alter the fact that it had been an elementary school.

At last, Finley's message was echoed by the one person who could make it stick: his president and CEO, Paul Lintner.

There can be little doubt that ESI's predicament had, to a certain degree, been enabled by U.S. National Bank. The close personal and working relationship over the years between Doug Strain and John Elorriaga had been a great benefit to the company. It came at a cost, however, and by 1981 that cost was coming due, and at a higher and higher interest rate. As late as May 1981, U.S. National Bank had agreed to raise ESI's line of credit to $20 million. Even Strain himself knew that additional funding had to come from somewhere else. But where?

Groceries and State Farm

Doug Strain and his family lived on a hill. On the same hill lived a woman whom for many years Doug would often help as she struggled to get her groceries up to her house. He would pick her up and bring her home, and even help her get her groceries into the kitchen. They would chat, and she told him that her son worked for State Farm Insurance. "Okay," Doug thought, "he works for State Farm." No big deal. Then one day:

I was delivering groceries one day and here was her son, Jim Bates, visiting his mother and thanking me, you know, for bringing groceries in, and we got to talking. He was aware of a lot of the young companies around here. So he was aware of us and said, "You wouldn't happen to be looking for money, would you?" And I said, "As the matter of fact, yes."

Jim Bates, it turned out, was not just an insurance agent, or a regular executive with State Farm, but was the head of a venture capital fund that worked very closely with State Farm's pension fund. State Farm was one of a handful of major U.S. companies, the most prominent of which was General Electric, that structured their pension funds to include a venture capital fund. Since venture capital was so speculative, companies preferred to keep it at arm's length from their pension funds. Jim Bates worked out of Chicago, and specialized in small companies, finding good prospects in need of capital, hooking them up with State Farm or G.E., and working with them to get to the $50 million level, and then helping them go public. If Bates did his homework, it was a win-win proposition: cash-strapped small cap companies got the boost they needed, the pension funds got an equity position in the companies and cashed in when they went public.

It was Jim Bates who introduced Doug Strain and ESI to Eberstadt Investment Company, in 1980. While Bates arranged a $5 million shot of capital for ESI, he also worked with Eberstadt and ESI to think in terms of a secondary offering of ESI's private shares. By the spring of 1981, Eberstadt began to line up a small group investors to add to State Farm's investment. The $5 million from State Farm could not have come at a better time, moreover, since it arrived precisely when ESI began its negotiations with Palomar in the fall of 1981. That November, Eberstadt informed ESI that it had located six investors willing to buy 24,000 shares of common stock in ESI. In a special meeting, the board approved the sale, amassing the 24,000 shares by allocating 4,000 treasury shares and buying 20,000 from current shareholders willing to sell back some of their holdings.

Among those most eager to sell shares back to the company was Merle Morgan.

Morgan was in the process of a phased retirement from ESI. As a major shareholder, Morgan's desire to divest himself of his ESI shares had for some time posed a dilemma to the company, since to redeem his shares would have placed a very serious additional burden on the company. Thus, various forces had combined by the winter of 1981-1982 to bring ESI to a delicate moment. An increasing number of employees were shareholders in the company. But in fact there was no market for their shares, save the company's own willingness to redeem them. With the voracious appetite for capital that came from its breathtaking growth, its expansion into European and East Asian markets, and its never-ending need for additional research funds to stay ahead of the competition, ESI had tapped out local lending sources. Taking on additional investors was the only answer.

The importance of ESI's relationship with Jim Bates and State Farm, not only for ESI but for other companies in the area cannot go unrecognized. First, it is so clear that often it is the little things that count, that take the measure of a person. When he was very young, and repairing radios and appliances in the back of Jack Murdock's store, Howard Vollum fixed a woman's vacuum cleaner. He told her that if anything were to go wrong with it, he would stand behind his work and fix it again. Over the years, several times, even as president of his own company and a man of considerable means, Vollum honored that promise, calling on the woman at her home to fix that vacuum. No fanfare, it was just the right thing to do. Howard and Doug were alike in this respect, since neither man needed much attention when they did the right thing. In building a relationship with Jim Bates and State Farm, Doug Strain began to feed Bates the names of other ventures in the area that could use Bates' help. From businesses like Precision Cast Parts on one end of the spectrum to educational institutions like Oregon Graduate Institute on the other, Strain's quiet work with Jim Bates brought millions of dollars into Oregon. One person who did notice Doug's work was Dave Bolender. From his perspective as president of Pacific Power, as a member of the Oregon Economic Development Commission and the State Transportation Commission, Bolender saw the effects of Doug's work everywhere he looked:

> One thing that Doug has never gotten credit for that I think he deserves is how much money he's brought into the State of Oregon.... [P]eople just absolutely don't understand how much he brought in through his personal relationship with Jim Bates and State Farm, just because Doug had the future of Oregon in mind. Bates brought an enormous amount of money into the state back at a time when we really needed it..., because of Doug's personal recommendations.

Going Public with a Mao Hat

At a special meeting on February 22, 1982, the ESI Board of Directors approved a secondary offering of ESI shares. Besides the Palomar shareholders who saw their equity transferred into ESI shares, Eberstadt presented six non-participating shareholders: Hartford National Bank, Kerry Lake Co., Kistler Associates, Robert R. Baker & Co., State Farm Insurance Co., and the University of Rochester. The new shareholders could take pleasure in a variety of positive factors. ESI's overseas operations were going well, not only in Europe, where the new British and French subsidiaries were coming on line, but in Japan as well. At ESI itself, a variety of advanced managerial techniques were also coming on line: after considerable planning, Manufacturing Resource Planning (MRP) and the PAL (quality circles) projects were in place. By the fall of 1982, Vice-President of Finance Finley projected consolidated sales of $43 million for fiscal 1983, a figure tantalizingly close to the magic $50 million Jim Bates liked to see before implementing a public stock offering.

Over the past few years, the growing complexity of ESI, its global reach, and the diversity of its product line all contributed to the increasingly complex administrative structure of the company. Housed in the remodeled but still relatively Spartan surroundings of the "schoolhouse," ESI's administrative team reflected the increasingly complicated nature of the company's business:

Chairman	Doug Strain
President & Chief Executive Officer	Paul Lintner
Executive Vice President	Lawrence Rockwood
Vice President, Finance	Dean Finley
Secretary/Treasurer	Charlie Davis
Vice-President, Systems Development	Ed Swenson
Vice President, Systems Operations	Mike Ellsworth
Vice President, Manufacturing	Wally Masters
Vice President, Instrument Business Unit	Jim Currier
Vice President, European Operations	Heinrich Stenger

In January 1983, in the company's very first published quarterly report, the figures looked particularly good. Based on the past year's 250% growth in European sales and likewise the 1000% growth in Japanese sales, expectations ran high. Indeed the board, at its quarterly meeting later in the month heard that things looked bright on through 1987. According to Lintner, however, there was one serious problem: how to restructure the company's $10 million debt? Lintner's comments and the ensuing board discussion signaled the beginning of a new era:

> Various alternatives were discussed for gradual purchase of some ESI stock that present stockholders wish to sell, including the employee stock option trust [ESOT]. Without a market for the stock, ESI directly or indirectly becomes the source of funds for stock transfers. On motion of Paul Lintner, seconded by Charles Davis, the officers will develop and present at the next meeting a four or five year plan for public offering of ESI stock.

Discussion of a public offering was by no means limited to the board meeting, and continued throughout the highest levels of the company on into the spring of 1983. "One of ESI's major shareholders" (Merle Morgan) made no bones about the fact that there should be a market in ESI shares, and that perhaps this meant the company should register for over-the-counter stock transactions. Finley estimated that it would take upwards of $30 million and five years for the company to cash out present shareholders. Still, there were those who resisted the idea of a public offering.

The alternative to a public offering seemed to be to find a major partner that would bear the spiraling costs of research and development. That idea was kicked around during the late spring and summer of 1983. But by August, the collective vision of senior management and board members had come into focus and the answer was clear: a pub-

Ed Swenson (left) explains an early version of ESI's revolutionary linear motion laser beam positioning system to a visibly astonished group of visitors in the winter of 1983.

lic offering. At its August meeting, on a motion by Charlie Davis and seconded by Rocky Rockwood, the ESI board approved the sale of 'shares of common stock of the company having an aggregate purchase price of up to $25 million." Current shareholders could offer as much as $7 million of the total. During the next ten weeks the lights burned very late at the schoolhouse as the myriad of details came together. Existing ESI stock was revalued; it split 12:1; employees received additional options; the Stock Purchase Loan Fund was increased from $400,000 to $1 million, to enable employees who were granted additional options to exercise those options. And there was more: the U.S. National Bank would serve as transfer agent; changes in the By-Laws; and registration with the Securities and Exchange Commission. Throughout the fall, Eberstadt helped guide the process, aided by the good offices of Hambrecht & Quist from San Francisco.

Late in the process, however, things bogged down. The Eberstadt people, the Hambrecht & Quist people, ESI's counsel, Henry Hewett, and Dean Finley had all gathered at the offices of Stoel Rives in downtown Portland. Paul Lintner was at home, where he and his wife Carol were entertaining Walter "Skip" Porter, one of the key people in ESI's collaboration with Texas A&M and a recent addition to the ESI board. The phone rang and Paul took a call from Dean. When Paul hung up, he indicated that he had to go down to Stoel Rives and asked Porter if he would like to come along:

> "Why don't you come and join me?" Paul said. "The lawyers are arguing over adjectives down there." So as we were leaving Paul's, I stuck my Mao hat that I'd got in China in about 1979, in my pocket.
> So we got up to the top of the Stoel Rives building, and Eberstadt had their Wall Street guys and Hambrecht & Quist had their Wall Street guys, and there must have been forty people, all in their thirteen-piece New York suits. Finley came out to kind of greet us and brief us on the situation: you know, they're down to intellectual bumbleshoot. So I just dropped back and let Paul and Dean walk in the conference room and I'm saying to myself, "Hell, I'm going to just see if I can't break this thing up."

Walter "Skip" Porter, one of ESI's earliest outside Board members, indeed at present the company's longest-serving outside Board member; scientist, academician, raconteur, and fly fisherman.

So I reached in and grabbed my Mao hat and put it on. And I came in far enough behind – everybody thought the group was in, and then another image appeared. And they all kind of looked at me and I said, "I understand there's a fire going on in here, and we're going to have a Chinese fire drill and get this thing put out." This guy, a kid of no more than twenty-four, but already on to it, said, "I don't think we've caught the full flavor of this company yet!" And in about fifteen minutes the whole deal was finished.

I thought it was very ironic that a Mao hat from Communist China helped to get a free enterprise deal done.

Details ironed out, officers of the company took the ESI story on the road, both domestically and in Europe. In the end, the underwriters were all domestic. Registered with the S.E.C. were 1.38 million shares of common stock, of which 840,000 were offered by the company, 360,000 were offered by existing shareholders, and 180,000 represented options exercised at the time of offering. On October 19, 1983 1.2 million shares of ESI were publicly offered at $15.00 per share

Everyone at ESI had reason to celebrate. And as the champagne corks popped that New Year's, Paul Lintner and his crew could reflect on a breathtaking several years. Projections for 1984 looked robust. Sales in Europe continued to improve; ESI KK in Japan was taking off. The Palomar line of products was outselling sales forecasts, even in Europe. Escondido needed more space. In fact, late in the year Palomar itself acquired a small start-up front-end chip capacitor manufacturer. So as the January meeting of the board came to an upbeat conclusion, everyone agreed that for their next meeting the board should gather at Palomar in April.

After all, San Diego would be such a delightful change from the cold and the rain of the typical Oregon spring.

UNFRIENDLY SEAS 1984 – 1993

The Captain and the Admiral.

The Death of the Helmsman

Doug Strain loved to sail. While one could hardly refer to a youngster born in Eastern Washington and raised in Idaho and Eastern Oregon as nautical, once he settled in Portland, he began a love affair with sailing. And as with any of his passions, Doug loved to talk to others about sailing, and loved even more introducing friends and colleagues to the water. Over the years, Paul Lintner had become one of Doug's favorite sailing partners, and so it was completely natural that following the ESI board meeting in San Diego on Thursday, April 26, 1984, the two went sailing on Friday.

The board meeting had gone well. The Portland contingent enjoyed getting to know the Palomar folks better and seeing the Escondido facilities. Palomar machines were selling well, especially in Europe, and discussion at the meeting concerned expanding Palomar's facilities to handle their increase in business. In the end the board approved the acquisition of a plot of land for new construction. On Friday, board members and their spouses went in various directions, some taking advantage of Southern California's many attractions, others heading home. And the chairman and his president went sailing. That night Paul and Carol Lintner had dinner with Dean and Nancy Finley at a Mexican restaurant in Old Town San Diego, "and, you know," recalled Finley, "we waved good-bye that night...."

The next morning, Saturday the 28th, Paul Lintner began his day with a run on the beach. He never returned. While on his run, Paul suffered a massive coronary and died. The job of telling people of the tragedy fell to Paul's best friend, Ed Swenson. "I was in bed Saturday morning, just kind of waking up. And the phone rings, and Carol is on the phone and said Paul had died. I was the first one she called. I had to call the rest of the executive committee and tell them. We were all in a state of shock." Charlie Davis had stayed behind in Portland, to entertain a visiting Chinese delegation from the electronics industry. Ed reached Charlie just before he was to head up the Columbia Gorge with his guests. Throughout that baleful day, Ed made his calls. Some were still nearby; he reached Dean Finley at Dean's parents' house in nearby Corona. The Rockwoods had gone for a nature hike out by the San Diego Zoo, and learned late that afternoon when they returned. Others had already arrived home; Ed reached Skip Porter in College Station, Texas: "Paul's dead. He died of a heart attack jogging on the beach."

Word made its way slowly around the company. Charlie Davis had to reach Larry Rapp in Germany, where Rapp was visiting ESI GmbH. "Drop your trip and get on the next plane home," Rapp recalled Davis' instructions. As one person called another, the impact began to sink in. "It just took the wind... kicked me in the stomach," said Armen Grossenbacher. Both Don Cutler and Dick Harris got word from Tom Richardson, and both engineers were worried. The future suddenly seemed so uncertain. Dick Harris remembered his anxiety: "Here was a guy that was heading up our company, really taking us into a future with a lot of growth potential, and now he was gone. What was going to happen?" From the top of the company to the shop floor, Lintner's death was not only a personal shock, but cause for grave concern. "He was a person that I and others had a lot of trust and confidence in," Cutler would say, "and now we were rudderless."

It was that sense of the captain and his ship that carried through ESI's grieving, and the celebration of Paul Lintner's leadership. The painful days of the following week were broken by a memorial service attended by virtually every single ESI employee. In his remarks, Doug Strain, facing the prospect of stepping into the breach to fill in for his fallen comrade, recalled his captain:

> Paul enjoyed sailing and I would like to use the metaphor of Paul as a sailor in this personal tribute to my true friend and trusted colleague of twenty-five years.
>
> Most skippers like to be always hard on the wind, spray breaking over the bow, sheets taut around groaning winches, much shouting into the wind on the part of the helmsman as he vigorously directs the crew in a series of less than perfect tacks he unrelentingly demands.
>
> Then there is the skipper like Paul who is expert at downwind sailing. When you come about from a hard beat upwind and the boat heads downwind, suddenly everything becomes calm and serene aboard as the boat nearly matches the speed and direction of the wind. The spinnaker is broken out and soon has the craft surfing down the faces of the waves giving the skipper and all of his crew an exhilarating downwind ride.
>
> In downwind sailing nothing seems to be going on, but in truth a great deal is happening. Such orders as there are given in a casual tone of voice and only the hiss of the water flashing along the hull reveals the tremendous speed the boat has attained.

The skipper is relaxed but alert with a light and sensitive hand on the tiller. There is even time for one of the crew to go below and brew up a pot of coffee in the galley....

And so it was that Paul's unusual downwind sailing has allowed the good ship ESI to pull out in front of the fleet and be first to discover some exciting new areas of technology and win more than its share of competitive races in the bargain.

The grace and skill with which Paul has sailed our ship the past five years has made us all proud to be aboard.

Now that our skipper has reached his own safe harbor we will long remember him for his championship sailing.

Privately, Paul's death hit Doug Strain harder than most people knew. People understood that Doug had waited many years to find the right person to step into his shoes, and that he was ready to disengage from the operations of the company. What they did not know, and what Doug confided to Carol Lintner in one of his many notes to her in the days following Paul's death, was that after twenty-five years Paul had become more than "a partner and a peer," to Doug, but like a son:

> As we dreamed a little, schemed a little, argued a little, and accomplished a lot together, our lives became related like right and left hands. While one hand was playing the melody the other was doing the counterpoint. Sometimes the right hand wasn't quite sure what the left hand was doing, but after 25 years we made some pretty good music together and could do some improvisation to cover each other if we had to.

Paul Dodson Lintner was by no means perfect. A good listener, a consensus builder, a leader who inspired those around him with his quiet confidence and his willingness to let the "buck stop here" with him, he also struck many who worked with him as somewhat remote, at times diffident, and certainly capable of manipulating others to accomplish what he felt was best. Somehow, though, with Paul, even the manipulation fit within the framework of superior management. Everything Doug Strain had said about Paul's management skill was true, and he had enjoyed the great good fortune of "sailing downwind." There is no way of knowing what kind of a skipper Paul Lintner would have been in heavy weather, but one thing is certain: he would have sailed with a seasoned and devoted crew. As it was, his untimely death had a paralyzing effect. "It was a company tragedy," lamented Dean Finley in 1998, "a disaster, just the worst possible thing that could have happened to ESI."

Coming About

For years ESI had enjoyed the luxury of making relatively leisurely key decisions. Not since the fire in 1957 had the company faced such a sudden emergency. And while insurance and the enormous goodwill of the community hastened ESI's recovery from the fire, in the spring of 1984 the company's loss was substantially different. Nevertheless, certain verities prevail. One such truth, whether within a family, a business or a community, is that the most critical decisions after a trauma are best postponed until the shock has worn off. ESI was all three – family, business and community – to its employees, and the task of moving forward placed immense stress on all those involved.

To fill the void in daily operations, Strain, Rockwood, Davis, Finley and Swenson took on additional responsibilities. Chief among Doug Strain's duties was the task of finding a successor to Paul Lintner, a job that Strain accepted with little relish and continuing sadness. Working on behalf of the board, by May Strain began to cast a wide net, using his own nationwide contacts and even outside agencies in hopes of turning up suitable candidates to succeed Lintner. By early June, the difficulty of the task had become clear: there were not that many qualified individuals expressing an interest in coming on board.

The ESI Board of Directors gathered on June 22 and 23, 1984, for a series of intensive meetings at the Jantzen Beach Thunderbird Hotel to interview prospective candidates. If there was a shared bias among board members, it seemed to be in favor of an outside candidate. As a first step, however, the board held lengthy individual interviews with the entire ESI senior management team. If an internal candidate were to surface, this was the time and place. There was indeed a certain subtle momentum behind an internal candidate. The company had always been run by members of the ESI family, first its founders and then Paul Lintner. The culture of ESI had evolved over thirty-five years. Those who fashioned and nurtured the culture believed with good reason that ESI's success was a function of that culture. So who better to continue this success story than someone from within?

On the face of it, there would appear to have been a handful of viable internal candidates. Yet as so often is the case, despite the continuity that an internal candidate brings, each strength seems offset by weakness, no matter how familiar. Davis had no desire for the job, and was soon headed for another term as State Utilities Commissioner. In Rockwood's case, retirement was imminent. Dean Finley had only been with ESI since 1979, and had no technical or marketing background. Despite his recent success with Palomar, Jim Currier's record was not a sustained one. The only other member of the senior management team who merited consideration was Ed Swenson. To many, Ed seemed an intriguing possibility. His vision and drive, ably supported by a cast of brilliant engineers, had meshed so smoothly with Paul Lintner's style. Yet more than once, Ed's vision of the company's future had clashed with that of Doug Strain. It was Lintner who had finessed these differences, balancing ESI between its past as an instruments company and its future as a systems company. In no small measure, people's admiration for Paul Lintner came because of his intuitive ability to balance these disparate elements in ESI's growth. In the end, it was Ed Swenson's unalloyed passion for systems that precluded his chances as an internal candidate.

The board's gentle bias toward an external candidate had not prevented it from hearing and considering possible inside candidates. When that failed to produce a clear successor to Paul Lintner, discussion returned to outside possibilities. The only problem was, the previous two months had failed to produce an attractive pool of candidates. Going into the board's meeting, both Strain and Davis had grown more and more worried. Doug had intended to step aside as Chairman within the next several years, passing the gavel to Lintner; Paul's death had not changed his mind. So in the back of Doug's mind, the right person would be one who could be president and chief operating officer for a few years while Doug remained chairman, and then move into the position as chairman when Doug bowed out. As Doug and Charlie mulled this over, during late May and early June, Doug had an idea.

Bill Walker, ESI board member, seemed like a possibility. He was not exactly an external candidate, nor on the other hand was he an internal one either. Certainly, as a board member he knew the ESI culture, and this would put him at ease with the old hands. An engineer who had risen through the ranks to become the head of the special research laboratory at Tektronix, he had the technical and managerial background ESI had hoped to find. He was a long-standing friend of the company, active in the same local and national technical and management associations to which Strain, Rockwood, Davis and Swenson belonged. In short, he was well-known, well-liked and well-respected. And, to Doug's surprise, when he began to feel Bill out, he indicated that he was ready for a change.

As a member of the ESI board, Bill Walker was in an uncomfortable position during the meetings of June 21st and 22nd. He was absent for the general discussions on the 21st that led into the individual meetings with senior managers. On the 22nd, however, Bill was in attendance. By the end of that day, it was clear that the board had no clear candidate, at which point the full board appointed Strain, Davis, Porter and Walker to develop additional candidates. Within a week, Strain, Davis and Porter asked Walker if he would consider the job. Hesitant at first, after some further discussion, not only with Doug, but with his old mentor Howard Vollum, Bill Walker accepted, becoming the forth president of ESI.

Bill Walker

Bill Walker was born in 1930 on a little farm in the Missouri Ozarks. This was an impoverished part of the country, and the Walker farm was no exception, "a little forty-acre rock farm," as he describes it. Walker loved those mountains, and remains, almost seventy years later, "still a hillbilly at heart." There was a spark in that hillbilly, though. He graduated high school at sixteen, and a year later had earned his teaching certificate. For three years he taught grade school, first through fourth grades, in a one-room schoolhouse. "There were three board members and they said they had just put a new roof on the schoolhouse and they didn't want any of the kids tromping around on the roof. That was the extent of my job description."

In 1950, during the Korean War, he joined the Air Force. It is a story common to so many Americans during the Forties and Fifties: whether drafted or enlisted, a generation of boys and young men left home, saw more of the world, and consequently lived different lives. Those different lives would change American society and American industry. Bill Walker's experience could be an archetype of the experience shared by millions of other men and women of his generation. In the Air Force Bill tested into electronics, went to fundamental and advanced radar school, on to the radar instructor school, and ultimately taught electronics and radar at Keesler Air Force Base.

As young radar trainees, Walker and his classmates were introduced to their first Tektronix oscilloscopes. For Walker it was love at first sight, and it led him to pursue a career in electronics. Discharged in 1955, he headed straight for the University of Missouri and a "double E' degree in electrical engineering. His sights set on Tektronix, Walker headed west, taking a job with Boeing so that he could be nearer his goal. Within six months, he had interviewed with Tek and landed a job in the test and calibration department. From there, Bill's skills, not only as an engineer, but as a manager,

Bill Walker, Executive Vice President and Chief Operating Office at Tektronix, and ESI Board member, agreed by the end of June 1984 to become ESI's new president following the sudden and tragic death of Paul Lintner.

attracted the attention of his superiors, not the least of whom was Howard Vollum himself. Walker's success in spearheading Tek's integrated circuit project in the Sixties was a key factor in Vollum's promoting Walker to Chief Engineer at Tektronix. By the early 1980's, Walker was Executive Vice President and Chief Operating Officer, sharing senior managerial duties with Tek's President, Earl Wantland, who was Chief Executive Officer.

The Eighties proved a difficult decade for Tektronix. There was no unified vision for Tek's future. Fiscal, marketing, engineering and organizational challenges combined to create both centripetal and centrifugal forces on the company. On the one hand, decentralization, or "divisionalization," seemed the answer; each segment of the company stood on its own feet, budget and all. On the other hand, however, there were powerful reasons to have a centralized engineering effort, encompassed in Tek Labs, so as to coordinate engineering and minimize fiscal and technological redundancy. Earl Wantland and Bill Walker did not exactly see eye-to-eye on these issues. So in the weeks after Paul Lintner's death, as Doug began to talk with Bill about Paul's successor, Bill listened:

> Doug and Charlie began to make a real push on me, and I was not very interested in doing it, honestly. I was really tired... I was still in the middle of the wars [at Tek], and I was very tired. I was really looking forward to bringing things [at Tek] to some kind of reasonable conclusion at that time. I was almost fifty-five and really ready to retire from Tek. I was getting very busy; my son-in-law and daughter were starting a business on the East Coast, and I was quite involved. So I wasn't very enthusiastic about this idea [of being Paul Lintner's successor at ESI]. But, you know, I thought about it. It seemed like probably a reasonable thing to go in there, and I said, well – I finally said – well, I talked to Howard about it quite a bit because I wanted him to feel good about why I might jump the boat from Tektronix. I felt an obligation there, so I talked with him about it, and he said, "Bill, you know, I think maybe you just might go and do that." So I finally told Charlie I would do it. But I said I really only wanted to do it for two or three years at the outside.

By the end of June 1984 Bill Walker felt really good about coming to ESI. He admired the people at ESI, and was especially loyal to Doug. He had a good working relationship with Charlie Davis, Ed Swenson and Mike Ellsworth. Bill respected ESI's vision: their unwavering commitment to standards and quality. And he respected ESI's ability "to scramble," to make things happen. If ESI had a weakness, it was marketing. Walker felt that as far back as the ESIAC, marketing had limited the company's success. Recently, however, sales had taken off so well, that this appeared nowhere near the problem it had been. In fact, for the 1985 fiscal year, sales were projected at $53,645,000, a significant increase over earlier projections.

By July 1984 Bill Walker had taken the tiller. As a board member and long-time friend of the company, it felt "like a family group... a nice family." At first, things went well. Fiscal 1985 turned out as strong as projected. A slight decline in European sales was more than compensated for by steady increases in Japan. Palomar sales were on target, as was the Escondido building project. Time and resources were even available to devote to ESI's memorial to Paul Lintner, a science education center in Washington County to be known as the Lintner Center. There was one problem, though. The crisis surrounding Paul Lintner's death and the search for a new president had revealed a weakness of ESI's Board of Directors. For some time the ESI board had felt the need for additional outside members but had been unsuccessful in finding any. A nominating committee of the board recommended retaining a search firm, Korn/Ferry Inc., to find "one or more persons" to join the board. And the board knew precisely the person(s) they were looking for: "such a person(s) would have special knowledge and experience, in order of importance: International business experience; Acquisitions/strategic growth planning; Experience operating a larger company; Technical savvy with a view of business horizon ten years ahead; Financial base with knowledge of financing miracles for a growth company." Not surprisingly, during the next several years, Korn/Ferry was unable to locate just such a person.

Buoyed by a healthy order backlog during early 1985 Walker began to implement new strategies and organizational changes he believed were necessary to move ESI "from a $5 million company to a $20 million company." Invariably, experience is an irresistible teacher. Thus, to no one's surprise, Bill began to import certain concepts from his long and illustrious experience at Tektronix. Divisionalization, which seemed to make such good sense at Tektronix, did not work as well at ESI. Perhaps it was a matter of scale, perhaps it was a deeper matter of institutional culture. What seemed to grate on managers and vice presidents was the unmistakable sense that they were all competing for their budgets. This was new, and somehow felt alien. Furthermore, Dean Finley, never comfortable playing the bad guy, was ill at ease within Walker's system of competing fiscal units. For both Walker and Finley this was a delicate problem, since, truth be told, there were those, Swenson or Currier, for instance, who were gifted in their entrepreneurial skill, while in the rough and tumble of competition, others came out feeling short-changed. In the end, no one was very happy.

Heavy Weather

Competition among internal business units might have made sense if orders kept cascading in. More money is a balm for most wounds. But in the winter of 1985, the mariner's rhyme began to come true: "Red skies at night, Sailors delight. Red skies in morning, Sailors take warning." The rosy sunsets of the previous decade suddenly gave way to a blood-red sunrise: domestic orders began to fall off. Briefly, minds focused on other things. At first the coming storm was masked by continued order volume from abroad. Of particular note was ESI's growing business in China. While the laser trimming business continued to grow in Japan, in China the rapid development of the national telephone network created a vibrant market for ESI's chip capacitor equipment. The Chinese market, moreover, involved not single sales, but entire factories, "turnkey factories," that integrated products from both ESI and Palomar. In an effort to beef up domestic sales, ESI created a leasing format that would allow start-ups and small companies that otherwise would have been priced out of systems equipment to acquire the needed technology.

As for the Board of Directors, two new members, John Elorriaga and Jack Kilby, joined the board by the end of 1985. Elorriaga, long-time friend of Doug Strain and banker to the company was no surprise. Kilby, on the other hand, was a figure of considerable significance. It was Kilby who, as a young engineer at Texas Instruments in 1958, invented the integrated circuit. Skip Porter had worked with Kilby at Texas Instruments. Though Porter eventually left TI to create the high technology lab at Texas A&M, he remained in close contact with his mentor Kilby. It was through Porter's contact, then, that Kilby agreed to join the ESI board.

In November 1984 Doug Strain passed the gavel to Bill Walker as Chairman of the ESI Board of Directors.

Jack Kilby, inventor of the integrated circuit, joined the ESI Board in 1985.

As Elorriaga and Kilby came on board, Walker's organizational realignment continued. Jim Currier moved from the Instruments Business Unit to become Business Development Manager. Tim Krouse, who had established ESI KK in Japan and had been Vice President for Pacific Rim Operations became General Manager of the Passive Component Equipment Division. This left open the Pacific Rim slot, which Walker moved to fill by adding to Heinrich Stenger's plate. Stenger now became the head of a new International Division that included not just Europe, but the Far East as well. Clear to those following ESI's restructuring were two inter-related facets: Walker was indeed realigning the company along functional lines, and, perhaps more significantly, the most rapidly rising star on the horizon was Heinrich Stenger.

When Doug Strain introduced Bill Walker as president and CEO to employees in 1984, he highlighted Walker's experience: "It's nice to have a scout who has been down the trail before." One of the very real strengths that Bill Walker brought to ESI was his emphasis on engineering and his belief that "you engineer your way out of any market downturn." During 1985 and 1986, ESI poured it on. Building on previous successful models, the new 8000 Series Laser Processing System was the state of the art in memory repair, with a beam positioning accuracy to one micron, and a beam-to-work sub-system that provided for the alignment of the laser with actual work surface features. In resistance trimming, the improved Model 44 Laser Trimming System, evaporating resistive material with individual laser pulses to achieve the desired resistance, could process up to fifty resistors per second. For the hybrid trimming market, ESI introduced the Model 4000 Laser Trimming System. Hybrid trimming, with its emphasis on high throughput of thick-film resistors, was a new market for ESI, and the Model 4000 made use of a different beam-positioning system, a galvonometer or "galvo" system. Customers were interested in "throughput," or the speed with which systems could handle individual resistors, chips or silicon wafers. So during the mid-1980s, ESI engineers not only made use of various high-speed beam-positioning systems, they constantly re-engineered and improved the automated wafer-handling components of the laser systems. Even the laser itself was the focus of intense research and development, as ESI introduced a new compact air-cooled Q-Switched Diode-Pumped YAG Laser exclusively for memory repair. Developed in partnership with Spectra-Physics, the new diode-pumped laser offered customers phenomenal savings in power – from 3000 watts down to 100 watts, thus allowing the new laser to be air-cooled – and a lamp life that rose from a mere 500-700 hours to 10,000 hours. Finally, in an effort to stay on top of the passive component business, in December 1986 ESI purchased Metoramic Sciences, Inc., a leading producer of materials for the multi-layer ceramic capacitor industry. The Metoramic acquisition enabled ESI to gain a much deeper understanding of the materials development process and design production equipment that more precisely met the demands of its passive component customers.

Tension will always exist between engineering and marketing. When a down cycle comes, as it inevitably does, "engineering the way out" does not always work. On the other hand, "marketing the way out" does not always work either, if buyers are simply not there. By 1986, the figures told the story. The order backlog, which had peaked at almost $44 million in the third quarter of fiscal 1985, fell steadily until by the fourth quarter of fiscal 1986 it had shrunk to $11 million. Orders themselves followed a similar decline, as did net sales. Having hit a high in the fourth quarter of 1985 at $23.8 million, net sales fell by the first quarter of 1987 — late summer/early fall of 1986 — to $13.3 million.

It was against this backdrop that on September 12, 1986, Bill Walker had the sad responsibility of announcing ESI's first net loss as a publicly held company. "Although we are disappointed at the prospect of ESI's first quarterly loss since we became a publicly held company nearly three years ago," Walker's statement said, "we are encouraged by the order trend and remain cautiously optimistic regarding the balance of our fiscal year." That optimism was not born out, however, and for fiscal 1987 ESI reported its first net operating loss in thirty years: $4.9 million, for a per share earnings loss of $0.80. There was no longer any doubt: the semiconductor industry had entered a cyclical downturn, and ESI was part of that trend. Walker and his team resorted to a variety of cost-cutting strategies, including layoffs, plant closures, and a ten percent pay reduction. For a company whose recent expansion had included not only the Science Park campus, but buildings as far flung as the Cornell Business Center and facilities on Nimbus Ave. across from Washington Square, cutbacks, layoffs and constriction hurt. The pay reduction effected employees differently. Some chose shorter days, retaining a five day week, while others chose to work four full days. Some pretty good steelheading got done on those Fridays, and there were those who would agree with Armen Grossenbacher, that when they resumed a five-day week, they missed their unpaid fishing days.

Mutiny

Bill Walker had never intended that his tenure as president and chief executive officer of ESI would last for more than three years. Inheriting the company at a moment of intense grief and deep concern following the death of Paul Lintner, Walker's tenure also coincided with the crest of a growth wave in the semiconductor industry. Believing, as he did, "that ESI could move from a $5 million to a $20 million company," he undertook the organizational reform that he believed would serve as the basis of such growth. But organization and culture takes longer than three years to change, and after three years this work had just begun – and certainly not without controversy. In what was perhaps the most ironic note of all, moreover, during Bill Walker's tenure, even as he sought to reform ESI's structure, the company was singled out in the best-selling *The 100 Best Companies to Work for in America.* The authors, Robert Levering, Milton Moskowitz and Michael Katz, praised ESI for its work environment, its generous employee benefits and its corporate culture. And then came the collapse of the semiconductor market.

By 1986 Bill Walker thought he had found the man who could step in as ESI's next president and chief executive officer. That man was Heinrich Stenger. A contemporary of Swenson and ESI's engineering elite, Stenger began his relationship with ESI as the company's sales representative in Germany. Personable, eager, and a skilled salesman, from the outset Stenger impressed the home office in Portland. When the time came to form its own marketing and service subsidiary in Germany, ESI GmbH, Stenger naturally became its manager. Throughout the Seventies Stenger's operation grew, and by the early Eighties he had become Vice President for European Operations. As Walker reorganized ESI's business units, Stenger became first Vice President for Europe and Pacific Rim

The timing of *The 100 Best Companies* could not have been worse. In the mid-1980's ESI could hardly afford to rest on its laurels.

Joining Ed Swenson, Dean Finley and Mike Ellsworth were Tim Krause (top) and Wally Masters (center), all of whom agreed, balking at the prospect of Heinrich Stenger (bottom) as president of ESI.

Operations, and then, by September 1986 Vice President of the International Division. With this last promotion, Walker asked Stenger to move from Munich to Portland, and by early 1987, Stenger had relocated to Beaverton, just outside of Portland.

The winter of 1986-1987 was an especially delicate moment for ESI. Against the backdrop of orders and sales that seemed in free-fall, the company entertained new initiatives. ESI not only acquired Metoramic Sciences, it entered into a new sales agreement in Japan with Advantest Corporation for the exclusive right to represent ESI in Japan for the sale of the Model 8000 Series and a new system under development, known as the CASTLE project. Nagging problems remained: ESI continued to expend tremendous internal resources on the merger of the ESI Stock Ownership Plan (ESOP) with the ESI Profit Sharing Plan, a move required by the federal regulations governing publicly held companies. The Audit Committee of the Board had for some time been concerned with the finances of some of ESI's foreign subsidiaries, especially ESI KK in Japan, but also some irregularities in the European operation. Thus it was that Heinrich Stenger arrived at a low point in ESI's fortunes.

That low point was again confirmed by Walker, when he reported to the board on May 8, 1987 that ESI:

> ...is again experiencing a difficult year in FY 87 and there is no indication that lack of sales was due to poor products. No immediate improvement is seen in Asian operations and a flat 1988 in forecast for Europe.... First quarter shipments will be dependent upon new orders because the backlog of unfilled orders at the end of FY87 will probably be small.

As Walker indicated, there was no doubt ESI had competitive products. Indeed, the company was hard at work engineering the next generation of products. There was also no doubt that the global downturn in the semiconductor business cycle was out of ESI's control. There was also no doubt, however, that morale among ESI's management team had never been lower. By the spring of 1987, the cumulative effects of external market forces, two years of reorganization that fostered competition among ESI's business units, layoffs, cutbacks and salary reductions, and a growing dissatisfaction with Bill Walker's executive style had taken their toll. Troubles with the Martin Marietta internal accounting systems further chafed nerves already rubbed raw. Shortly after Heinrich Stenger arrived he summoned his financial lieutenant, Hans Schreckenmeuller, to join him in Portland. This did nothing to calm anxious souls in the schoolhouse.

Culture is one of those intangibles found in nations, societies and institutions, the roots of which are deep and tenacious. Bill Walker tried to change the culture at ESI, driving the company to the next level. The resistance he encountered was to be expected, frustrating, but hardly fatal. As it became clear in the late spring of 1987 that Walker intended to turn the reins of the company over to Heinrich Stenger, the cultural breach became too wide to bridge. To some this most complex chapter of ESI's history is its most glorious moment, for others it holds a more tragic meaning.

Stenger's drive and ambition combined with a leadership style that troubled many of his colleagues. For all of his gifts and European charm, Stenger alientated virtually every single senior executive at ESI with his Prussian style. And to many, the thought of Schreckenmeuller was even more unsavory. So, in their anxiety over the company's performance, out of a fear of Stenger's impending appointment, and out of their growing sense of resentment that Stenger's appointment was to be imposed rather than the result of a collaborative process, a handful of senior executives began to meet to discuss the future of the company. In what has come to be known within ESI as "the palace revolt," Ed Swenson, Dean Finley, Tim Krouse, Wally Masters and Mike Ellsworth formed the nucleus of an effort to resist the appointment of Stenger as president.

Charlie Davis was notably absent from these meetings. Davis was again on leave from ESI to serve as Public Utilities Commissioner in Salem. Davis was nevertheless drawn into the fray as a confrontation between the mutinous executives and ESI's board seemed inevitable. At the request of the group, and as a last resort, Davis undertook a kind of shuttle diplomacy, spending a weekend on planes and in airports, in an effort to convince those board members who lived out of the area that a crisis was at hand. As the result of Davis' efforts, the board gathered in Portland on August 15, 1987, to interview senior management of the company. At the Benson Hotel on the following day, after hearing from Bill Walker, the board discussed at length a variety of different succession and staffing options. Board members had not liked what they had heard. Persuaded that Walker's intention to appoint Stenger as president was probably not a good idea, the board was no less troubled by the revolt they had on their hands. Sensing the board's reluctance to endorse his initiative, Bill Walker resigned as president and chief executive officer on August 27th. Heinrich Stenger's resignation followed immediately.

As is frequently the case in rebellion, it is easier to know what to oppose than to have a program in its place. It was the board rather than the opposition that moved to fill the awkward void created by the August crisis. While each of the opposition could agree on their rejection of Walker and Stenger, none had a clear plan to the next step. Once again, ESI was in the unenviable position of having to choose its leader during a moment of acute trauma. Previously, feelings of grief and confusion followed in the wake of Paul Lintner's death and had cast a shadow on his successor. This time, resentment, exhaustion and anxiety permeated the deliberations.

The mutiny had been a culture war. The apparent victors were those old hands who fought to preserve the company as they knew and loved it. Faced with no palatable external alternatives, the board understood the need for an internal choice, a consensus-builder, a peace-maker. On August 29th ESI's board elected Mike Ellsworth president and chief executive officer.

Mike Ellsworth

Mike Ellsworth was born in 1943 in Portland into a middle-class Catholic family. In addition to his family, educational experiences at St. Thomas More Grade School, Jesuit High School and the University of Portland formed the young man. Private Catholic schools were financially taxing for the modest Ellsworth family. Mike's father was a sales manager at the RC Cola Bottling Company, and from the age of fourteen on, Mike worked at the bottling plant, contributing to his high school and college education. At the University of Portland, Ellsworth majored in engineering science, graduating with a BS in 1965. He took a job with Boeing and pursued a graduate degree at the University of Washington on the side. Tough going for a young man with a new family, so when Mike heard that Bell Labs had a program for people in exactly his position, he jumped at the chance:

Charlie Davis, who agreed to take the message of "the palace revolt" to the Board.

Mike Ellsworth, against the backdrop of a world map showing ESI's subsidiaries and marketing offices, seemed a natural successor to Bill Walker.

They had a program where they give you basically half-time off, pay you a full-time salary, and give you half-time off to get a MS degree. So I went to work for Bell Telephone Laboratories for a few years in Chicago, Illinois, at the Naperville facility. Indian Hills, it's called, and went to graduate school down at Northwestern and got an MS at Northwestern.

Both Mike and his wife were native Portlanders, and now with a second child, the couple longed to return home. So Mike started looking for opportunities in the Portland area. He found ESI, "interviewed with Rocky and Merle and some other people and went to work for ESI in 1969." Within a very short time, Mike found himself thrown into ESI's pioneering laser trimmer project. He was the project's mechanical engineer. By the beginning of the Eighties, Ed Swenson and Mike Ellsworth were, in effect, partners running the systems business. Paul Lintner made Ed vice president of the systems business unit, and Mike the general manager of systems. Save for titles, the two were peers, running the systems business unit together. Between them, Ed and Mike, encouraged by Paul Lintner, made a good team. Perhaps Mike's willingness to allocate resources to Jim Currier's Palomar project could frustrate Ed, but by the semiconductor decline of the mid-Eighties, as Palomar took off, the wisdom of developing this "third leg" of the ESI stool was born out.

By his own admission, Mike Ellsworth was a reluctant member of the those who met in the summer of 1987 in opposition to Bill Walker's plans for ESI. During Walker's tenure Mike had not developed the same concerns about the company's situation as had his fellow vice presidents. In fact, that summer Ellsworth spent much of his time tackling a crisis in Japan, where a major order for five complete laser systems seemed to be unraveling. In the end, the order held up. But upon returning home and learning of Walker's intention to appoint Heinrich Stenger as his successor, Ellsworth joined the rebellion. "You can't run a technology company like a strong German marketing company [where] control is everything," Ellsworth thought at the time.

Scholars of revolution invariably point to the single most dangerous moment in such cataclysmic events: what if the revolutionaries are successful? Then what? Who succeeds? And will his fellow revolutionaries accept his new authority? As Americans, we have been blessed: revolutions are not our specialty; we only needed one. It is not surprising, then, that when such events happen in institutions in this country, few if any are adequately prepared for the outcome. Mike Ellsworth had a sense of such perils, however dim that sense may have been at the time, and however clear it may have become in subsequent years. "I was afraid I would be asked [to serve as president] but I wasn't at all sure I wanted it. I wasn't sure I was ready, and I didn't know how the others would accept it." Mike Ellsworth, the reluctant Fletcher Christian, came to the bridge.

Upon assuming office, Ellsworth moved quickly to assure employees that ESI was in good shape. And, by all accounts, his selection was a popular one among members of the ESI family. "Mike Ellsworth was a person liked by all of the engineers... he was liked by everybody," recalled Larry Rapp. To Hollis Smith, Ellsworth "was just a real people person." In fact, long-time employee Joan Sulman seemed to speak for almost everybody when she recalled how relieved she was that Ellsworth had been appointed president: "I just remember I was awful happy when Mike was made CEO."

Not only was Mike Ellsworth a popular and reassuring choice, employees saw him as approachable, as one of them. When he was president, Doug Strain made a point of walking through the plant, chatting with everyone, staying in touch with the grass roots of the company. Slightly more distant, Paul Lintner made every effort to continue his mentor's habits of staying in touch with his extended family. By the time Bill Walker became president, ESI had grown to almost a dozen buildings, and such intimacy had become more difficult. Now, as ESI began to shrink, it became easier to move among the employees again, and Mike made every effort to do so. But these were difficult times, and the weight of the company's future would weigh heavily on his shoulders. It was a mark of the employees' relief that he was at the helm, however, that they felt comfortable in approaching him, even if it might be awkward. Gerda Woods, who had worked her way up at ESI from the lunchroom at the Macadam plant to one of the company's most accomplished purchasing agents, felt no compunction about stopping Mike and giving him some advice:

> One day he walked through the lunchroom, and we were sitting there. And a new employee was sitting there with me, and she wanted to know who he was. I said, "Oh, he's the president, that's Mike Ellsworth." And she said, "Are things that bad?" And I asked, "Why do you ask?" "Because he had a scowl on his face," she replied. In fact, I talked to him later, and I said, "Mike, you know when you walk through the lunch room, why don't you smile? People think we're in desperate straits here." "I had things on my mind," he replied.

Killer Bugs on Board

Mike Ellsworth did have things on his mind, and things really were that bad. By early 1988, it appeared that the semiconductor industry might be pulling out of its slump. Appearances were fleeting, however, and from mid-1989 until almost the mid-1990's, the industry drifted in the Horse Latitudes that becalmed virtually all of high technology at home and abroad. And Mike Ellsworth had the misfortune to arrive on the bridge at this very moment.

Industry-wide trends can wound companies and they can certainly shorten the tenure of executive officers. But ironically, this was only one of the problems Mike Ellsworth faced. And from time to time, it seemed like one of his lesser concerns. Most dramatic, and certainly most widely appreciated within the company, was the fate of its newest, next-generation laser system, the Model 9000. Beset in its early days by design and software problems — "killer bugs" —, the Model 9000 loomed as the company's most dangerous gamble. These "killer bugs" plagued the project for well over a year. But there were other killer bugs, less obvious but in many ways more pernicious, that plagued the company during the Ellsworth years. From the board on down there were bugs, and these bugs were in the fabric, the culture of ESI, where they had lain dormant during earlier, happier times. Now, in the wake of the tremendous stress of the struggle for the soul of the company in 1987, they began to hatch. How was the circle of senior managers, many of whom saw ESI in terms of his own contributions, going to react to Ellsworth's leadership? Who would chair the board now that Doug Strain had retired and Bill Walker had resigned? How would the board respond to Ellsworth and ESI's management team? And how would ESI finance its future if its flagship Model 9000 failed to live up to its promise? The answers, as Ellsworth was soon to discover, were hardly consoling.

As the semiconductor recession deepened in the late 1980's and as ESI's troubles multiplied, people could see Ellsworth's concern etched on his face.

Along with tapping Mike Ellsworth as president and chief executive officer, the ESI board had to choose a new chairman. At this point, Doug Strain, who had witnessed the recent uprising and for the most part had resisted being personally involved, stepped in to help find a new board chairman. With Walker's resignation, who among them would agree to chair the group, and at the same time who was acceptable to the group and to ESI's managers? In the fall of 1987, the consensus pointed to Skip Porter. As ESI's longest sitting outside board member, Porter had enjoyed a close relationship with Paul Lintner, was on very good terms with Ed Swenson, had the technical background to understand ESI's product development, and had the management skill to run a board. Doug called Porter to ask him to take on the job.

At first Porter begged off. He had just taken on a new challenge as founding president of the Houston Advanced Research Center Park, a consortium of Texas A&M, the University of Texas, Rice University and the University of Houston whose aim was to bring the super-collider to Texas. At the same time, Porter had agreed in 1987 to become a member of the American Leadership Forum. But Doug was persistent: "Look, we've gone through all this stress. We don't need any more stress right now. The board is saying they'd like you to be chairman. Do it for a year; buy us a little time. We will get you out of it in a year."

Doug's appeal to Skip Porter did not fall on entirely barren ground. Whether he knew it or not, Doug was working soil long ago cultivated by Paul Lintner. As Doug spoke, Skip's mind returned to the evening years earlier at his home in College Station in 1980 when Paul had come to invite him to become a member of ESI's board. In a conversation tinged with ironic portent, Paul made his pitch:

> We were sitting in my living room and I was taken by his request of me to make a lifetime commitment to remain affiliated with ESI. And I smiled at that and I said, "Well, you know, Paul, it's interesting, but hell, none of us knows how long we're going to live. You know, a lifetime commitment is a substantive request to make of somebody, and a substantive thing to agree to." So all of that flashed through my mind: Paul sitting in my living room asking me to make a lifetime commitment to the company.

Skip Porter agreed to serve for a year. He got permission from the board of the Houston Advanced Research Center and began his monthly commutes from Houston to Portland. In December 1987 he began a tenure that would stretch for far more than only a year, in the end lasting for the next five years, five of ESI's most difficult years.

Trade shows, such as the 1987 International Society of Hybrid Manufacturers (ISHM) seen here, were the ideal place to introduce new equipment.

Ellsworth and Porter worked closely together. The two moved quickly to rebuild morale, as Ellsworth reported to shareholders in 1988:

> … we believe that management should focus the efforts and energies of our employees to meet corporate objectives in the most efficient and profitable manner. To that end, we've restructured the company to reflect a more harmonious, less internally competitive environment, and one which fosters a new spirit of teamwork and cooperation among all our people.

And for a time things seemed to get better. In 1988 ESI's orders were up 33%, sales up 19% over the previous year. Coming off the net income loss in 1987 of $4.8 million, in 1988 ESI tabulated a small but satisfying income of $744,000, on net sales of $68.6 million. The figures for 1989 appeared to be even better. Net sales reached $83.1 million, producing net income of $6.3 million. Those with even a modest historical memory, however, could reflect on the fact that ESI had yet to rebound to the level of sales and net income recorded in 1985. Nevertheless, ESI's performance was cause for muted celebration, as reflected in the slow battle of ESI share values back from a third quarter low in 1988 of just under $6 per share, to a fourth quarter high of $13.75 in 1989.

Sadly, however, despite ESI's best efforts, the company's fate seemed to rest elsewhere, for in the second half of 1989, the brief expansion in the microelectronics capital equipment market came to a screeching halt. ESI's net sales began a three-year 30% decline that took them from $82 million in fiscal 1989 to $58.2 million in 1992. Share value followed suit, bottoming out in the fourth quarter of fiscal 1992, at $2.35 per share.

ESI's perilous decline from 1987 to 1992 was certainly heavily influenced by the brutal cyclical realities of the semiconductor industry. But other factors played their part. Those bugs, those killer bugs. Within the fabric of ESI's culture certain problems could no longer be ignored. And they began at the top, with ESI's board. For years ESI's board had been essentially passive. First Doug Strain, and then Paul Lintner had managed the board skillfully, keeping it at arm's length. Even with the addition of external members, the board was not heavily involved in ESI's fortunes. Bill Walker continued that tradition. When confronted by the mutiny of 1987, the board was forced to act. This was unfamiliar territory for most board members. And as a result of this crisis, ESI's board's subsequent response is hardly surprising: they wanted greater accountability and a closer rein on the company's affairs. For Ellsworth and Porter this would have posed no insurmountable problem, had the board been unified in its vision of where ESI should be

From crating to unpacking, from setting up to final display, the job of taking a system to a show, in this case the Model 4000 Laser Trimming System, represented a daunting task. Sometimes working with the convention center staff, sometimes despite them, the ESI team had to organize enough power and water on the floor of the trade show to make sure their system worked.

Board member Larry Hansen, one of the inventors of the microwave oven while at Litton Industries, and veteran executive at Varian, echoed the concern of others on the Board in the late 1980's that ESI had lost its strategic vision.

heading. But such was not the case. Serious divisions within the board emerged over technology development, corporate restructuring, finances and profitability.

Issues long unresolved, issues that could be finessed in good times, now surfaced, effecting the daily life of ESI from the boardroom to the shop floor. Was ESI an instruments company or a systems company? Could it be both? Indeed, should it be both? Were the internal fiscal and auditing controls equal to the grave challenge facing the company? Was the consensus management style that had been at the heart of the crisis of 1987 capable of meeting a sustained market downturn? These were high stakes, indeed, and employees could feel board members clamoring for answers. Doug Strain was deeply concerned about the future of the instrument business, moreover he had reservations about the future of systems. In regular receipt of Ed Swenson's bullish reassurances, however, Skip Porter and Jack Kilby were much more sanguine about the future of systems. With a thirty-year career at Litton and Varian behind him, board member Larry Hansen repeatedly called for a strategic vision. As for the more local board members, John Elorriaga and the recently arrived Ralph Shaw called for tougher fiscal management.

Nowhere were these tensions more clearly evident than in the case of the Model 9000 Laser Processing System, ESI's next generation memory repair system. As early as 1984 Swenson and Ellsworth and a small group of engineers in the Systems Business Unit began to brainstorm a new memory repair system. By 1985, encouraged by Bill Walker's commitment to new product development, a separate engineering project took shape outside the existing "box."

To this day opinions within ESI vary on the gestation and birth of the Model 9000. As ESI continued to refine the Model 80, which became the Model 8000, concerns arose that both domestic and foreign competitors might beat ESI to the punch with the next generation memory repair system. Of particular concern were the Japanese, specifically Nikon. As new "smart" machines began to roll off assembly lines – copiers, fax machines, printers, and high definition television – these machines would require more and more memory. The idea was to tap into the anticipated market for increased production yields and the increased capacity of memory components for memory-intensive computer and consumer electronics products.

There had been a clear progression of ideas and technology from the Model 20 all the way through to the Model 8000. Now the idea was to start from scratch, and to rethink things from the ground up. As continuous refinements appeared in the Model 8000, elsewhere, with little or no communication between projects, the Model 9000 began to take shape. Engineers on the 9000 wanted to set a new standard in speed and accuracy. Aiming for cutting at one-half micron, the 9000 team designed a system that would move, stop and position its beam, burn – or "blow" – a link in the redundant circuit, and then move to the next link: move, settle, blow; move, settle, blow. In the meantime, the Model 8000 team, denied the opportunity to work on the 9000, invented a different "blow on the fly" system that was many times faster than the 9000 target speed.

ESI unveiled the Model 9000 Laser Processing system at the SEMICON/West trade show in May 1988, under the slogan "poised for the future... working for you today." The first laser system designed from the ground up specifically for semiconductor memory repair, the Model 9000 at first was hardly "poised for the future" and did not work for anyone "today." From its first release, there were both hardware and software problems. In an attempt to bring the 9000 up to the speed and efficiency of the 8000, major engineering changes occurred late in the game, and the software problems seemed to go on forever. Once the 9000 hit the market, the tendency at ESI was to try not only to engineer but to program as many special or customized features into the 9000 as possible.

During the next eighteen months, ESI delivered 35 Model 9000 Laser Processing Systems, and 160 Model 8000 Laser systems for repairing one megabyte dynamic random access memories, or DRAMs. Bright spots continued to be Palomar's line of termination and test systems, particularly the Model 16 Rotary Test Sorter, as well as the ESI Model 4000A Laser Trimming System. One particularly bright spot was the emerging market in Korea, where ESI maintained a 100% market share in semiconductor systems. But the "killer bugs," the dozens and dozens of problems in the Model 9000, had spawned another, larger killer bug: that of funding.

If there were problems, or bugs, woven into the fabric of ESI, among the most pernicious was that of funding, specifically the capital expenditures necessary in research and development that enable a company to stay ahead of its competitors. By 1989 ESI was again on the lookout for outside funding sources to cover its research costs. In December 1989 the Technology Committee considered a proposal to CIBA-Geigy/Spectra Physics for funding a joint laser imaging project. On the same day, December 7th, the Finance Committee of the board had a no-holds-barred discussion of the company's financial performance, under the heading: **"Lack of 'Bottom Line' Financial Orientation."** Attending the meeting were committee members John Elorriaga, Skip Porter, Ralph Shaw and one of the newest board members, Dave Bolender. Also attending the meeting were Mike Ellsworth, Dean Finley and one of Finley's assistants from the Finance Department, Mark Shia. The discussion, summarized in the minutes by Mike Shia, reveals not only the deep consternation of those present, but the new penchant of the ESI board to micromanage the company:

- The financial performance of the Company has been inadequate since the Company went public. The poor financial returns have resulted in a low stock valuation.

- The management of the Company has an engineering orientation. It needs to develop a financial orientation, as well.

- Management and the Finance Committee need to evaluate the financial "worth" of each new product development program and each of the Company's major businesses – individually and in total. Decisions need to be made regarding which should be pursued and how they should be financed.

- The progress of each program should be continually monitored, from a financial standpoint, to determine if progress is being made according to plan.

- There are plenty of promising and challenging technical opportunities – we need to put the creative financing in place that will allow us to be successful.

- The Finance Committee needs to give direction in establishing the required rate of return for the Company and new business ventures that are evaluated.

- The cyclicality [sic] of the capital equipment business cannot be avoided. We should seriously consider diversification into "razor blade" types of businesses.

Decision:

The Finance Committee will need to play a major role in establishing realistic financial goals, evaluating the company's financial plans and business opportunities, and determining appropriate methods of financing both the

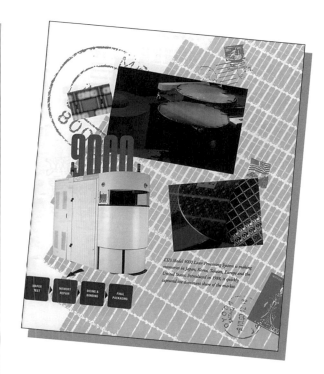

The 1990 Annual Report proclaimed that "ESI's Model 9000 Laser Processing system is making memories in Japan, Korea, Taiwan, Europe and the United States." Unfortunately, since its introduction in 1988, customers' memories of the Model 9000 were not all that positive. By 1992, however, the 9000's bugs had been eliminated, and the 9000 Series went on to become one of ESI's most celebrated systems.

For Chris Nawrocki the "killer bugs" on the Model 9000 were truly a nightmare. Ultimately the 9000 triumphed, and while he never threw in the towel, it appeared he brought one with him just in case.

ongoing operations of the Company and the promising new product development programs.

With the list of "killer bugs" of the 9000 stretching out indefinitely into the future, markets weakening, and engineering costs rising, the Finance Committee had every reason to be worried. The December 7th meeting had hardly been an endorsement of Mike Ellsworth and his team. At its March 1990 meeting the board heard Dean Finley "review specific plans for asset reductions and layoffs." But by now everyone at ESI, from the board down was increasingly worried about share value. It was cold comfort on September 27th, when Chris Nawrocki, Vice President for Operations, announced to the Technology Committee that the last item on the list of "killer bugs" for the 9000 had been fixed. "The committee responded with a round of applause." In actuality, the 9000 continued to cause trouble. As late as the spring of 1991, "reliability issues" remained "especially serious" at Texas Instruments, "where they have been concerned about equipment failures." Neither software nor hardware fixes seemed to be working, and "this is not acceptable to T[exas] I[nstruments]."

Dry Land

In the end, the Model 9000 Laser Processing System would become the industry standard. The bugs that plagued the system were fixed. But the project was a metaphor for ESI and its troubles in the late Eighties and early Nineties. By the summer of 1991, with more cuts in the offing and order flow very low, board members had become frustrated. "By that time, we were eating our seed corn," recalled Porter. Something had to be done.

One of the most persistent voices for action came from Ralph Shaw. A venture capital specialist who had moved from the East Coast to Portland, Shaw specialized in small cap start-up high technology companies. Nominated to the ESI board by John Elorriaga, Shaw joined Elorriaga in calling for sweeping fiscal change and tighter controls at ESI. At long last, it seemed that the fundamental question at ESI – was the company driven by engineering or the bottom line? – had come to the center of the stage.

Chairman Porter called a special board meeting for August 17, 1991, in Denver. In the end, neither Elorriaga nor Shaw nor Bolender were able to attend. Meeting at the Stouffer Concourse Hotel at the Denver Airport were Porter, Strain, Ellsworth, Kilby, Hansen, and Kenneth Olsen. Olsen was ESI's new chief financial officer, having succeeded the retiring Dean Finley some months earlier. Also present at the meeting was Ed Swenson, there to report on the status of the laser systems business and new customer opportunities.

The Denver meeting was a turning-point in the history of the company, not just for what was said at the meeting, but for what was left unsaid as well. Feelings ran high at the meeting, about the future of the laser systems business, about blunders in ESI's marketing strategy, and over matters of fiscal controls. Ellsworth and Swenson gave a presentation on the current status of the company, and possible future opportunities, a presentation that the board found "too general, and did not include specific action plans with dates, dollar amounts, and people assignments." And board members' concerns ran deeper:

> In addition, the opinion of the Board was that management's current view of products and markets is almost exclusively and inside-out look, i.e., first management decides what ESI's technology can do, and then they look at

where that technology can be sold. All agreed that a better approach would be to look at what kinds of good, strong markets exist, and then to look at how ESI could exploit those markets.

The tenor of the meeting was unmistakable: the Porter-Ellsworth team simply had to make the difficult decisions that would insure the company's survival. With no end to the global semiconductor recession in sight, not even a tough new marketing strategy held out much promise.

The microscope of hindsight is a wonderful thing. Through its lens events and their myriad causes stand out in relief, and we are able to make sense of the past. Such clarity is rarely, if ever, available to those caught up in the moment as the event itself unfolds. Having said that, however, it is important to note that few at ESI in the fall of 1991 were in any doubt that the future of the company hung in the balance. The company's performance and its plummeting share value forced ESI to confront long-postponed questions. The years of frustration with the Model 9000 and its problems raised doubts among even the most enthusiastic of the systems engineers: was ESI an instrument company or a systems company? "I have to admit," said none other than Don Cutler, ESI's most revered laser engineer, "that back in the days when they were trying to make the memory repair systems work, if it had been my decision, I don't think I would have gotten into that business." The development costs were so high, and the technical problems so daunting, memory repair was, in Cutler's words, "bleeding edge" technology, since it required such a large share of the company's resources. And in 1991, most people at ESI felt anemic.

With board support waning, Mike Ellsworth knew his tenure as president had run its course. Ralph Shaw had already departed the board. John Elorriaga, one of Doug Strain's and ESI's oldest and closest supporters, relayed the news that U.S. Bank would not loan ESI more money. On that note, Elorriaga sadly took his leave of the board as well. Through the gloom of that fall, Porter worked with Ellsworth to structure Mike's exit. At the same time, he was contemplating his own. In December Mike Ellsworth bowed out, and the board accepted his resignation on January 10, 1992. At that same meeting, Skip Porter offered his resignation as Chairman of the Board.

It was time for someone on the board to step up. Different voices within ESI clamored for different solutions. Ken Olsen's concern ran to how demoralized ESI's management team had become. With Palomar one of the only bright spots during the pervious five years, Jim Currier called for expanding Palomar's operations. Naturally, Ed Swenson appealed for just a little more patience with the memory repair line. Chris Nawrocki, on the other hand, wondered out loud whether ESI should exit the semiconductor market altogether. With the company on the very precipice, and with its founder and former chairman long past his own anticipated retirement, who could step up? Indeed, under these conditions, who would want to step up?

THE COMEBACK 1992–1999

More than any others, Dave Bolender (right) and Don VanLuvanee were responsible for ESI's remarkable turnaround in the 1990's.

Dave Bolender

In the winter of 1999, the Sunset Tunnel on Highway 26 in the Oregon Coast Range suffered a cave-in, killing one of the team of engineers from the Oregon Department of Transportation who were inspecting it. The tunnel was closed for more than six weeks for major structural repairs, during which time the Department of Transportation called for an independent investigation of the accident. The Department knew just whom to turn to: Dave Bolender. What was widely understood in Oregon in 1999 became apparent at ESI in 1992: if you needed a person on whose integrity you could absolutely depend in a time of great stress, Dave Bolender was your man.

Dave Bolender was born in 1932 outside Buffalo, New York, in the town of Hamburg. Raised in upstate New York, in 1950 Bolender won a scholarship to the Colorado School of Mines, one of the nation's leading technical colleges. Graduating in 1954 in petroleum engineering, he went to work for General Electric, in their nuclear power division at Hanford, Washington. While at Hanford, he broadened his engineering credentials with graduate study at the University of Idaho, specializing in nuclear engineering. In 1962, he left GE to work on the nuclear ship *Savannah*, an attempt to build a nuclear-powered commercial vessel, a combination passenger/cargo ship. When the government shut down the *Savannah* project, Bolender moved to Westinghouse, working on a variety of secret projects in Admiral Hyman Rickover's nuclear submarine program. Next, Bolender moved into Westinghouse's commercial International Division of Nuclear Energy, and eventually into non-nuclear power generation for Westinghouse. From Westinghouse, Bolender came to Pacific Power and Light, which in the Seventies was withdrawing from the nuclear power business, and Bolender became involved with the company's move into non-nuclear power generation, in particular their coal-fired operations.

At Pacific Power, the nuclear engineer Bolender absorbed the complexities of the utilities business, human relations, and management, rising to become president of Pacific Power. Under his leadership Pacific Power and Light grew and prospered, merging with Utah Power to become one of the region's most influential companies. In 1991, Bolender retired from Pacific Power, timing, as it happened, that was simply perfect for ESI.

Dave Bolender joined ESI's Board of Directors in 1988. By this time he had crossed paths with Doug Strain a number of times. Both served together on the boards of the Oregon Graduate Center and the U.S. Bank. Even after Strain retired from the U.S. Bank board, they had a mutual friend in John Elorriaga. Doug Strain recognized in Bolender just the kind of person ESI needed on its board, having had in the Eighties so much trouble broadening the board's membership. For his part, Bolender was fascinated by the older Strain. "He was more worried about [the year] 2050 than I was. He was a long-term thinker, enormously interesting," recalled Bolender. And it was Doug's down-to-earth manner that really attracted Dave: "Doug could get your interest up in lasers or other stuff that you didn't know a damn thing about and explain it in a way that didn't make you feel like you were an idiot. It's a rare combination to find somebody who reads technical magazines, you know, like they were comic books and yet is able to talk to anybody from a janitor to a CEO."

Bolender's affection for Doug Strain did not blind him to the challenges of serving on ESI's board. Arriving soon after the Ellsworth-Porter era began, Bolender found the board to be, in a word, "dysfunctional." He was troubled to find that, "there were camps, strong, strong camps." One of his concerns was the over-emphasis on technical detail at board meetings:

> It was so interesting. We would spend the whole day going over technologies and lasers and where the semiconductor business was going – should we even be in the memory repair business – that kind of stuff. And the problem that the place was crashing down around our ears would come up in the last twenty minutes. And be postponed.

Bolender nevertheless was patient, strongly committed to the principle that boards served as governors and management runs the business.

By 1991, as things came to a head at ESI, Bolender's retirement from Pacific Power and Light suddenly freed up his calendar for other challenges. He was willing to take on an increased commitment at ESI. Agreeing to follow Skip Porter as Board Chairman, Dave Bolender became ESI's fourth chairman in January 1992, with a mandate to find the company a new chief executive officer. Dave's first act was to assure the company that "there will be no further changes before a new CEO is hired."

A nuclear engineer and consumate executive, Dave Bolender retired as President of Pacific Power in 1991. Already four years on the ESI Board, Bolender was an ideal successor to Skip Porter as Chairman of the ESI Board.

Good Timing and a Good Search

Whether investing in the market or preparing a gourmet meal, setting the hook in a steelhead or coaching a team to peak at the right point in the season, timing is everything. There is no doubt, that Dave Bolender was the right man, at the right time. His arrival as board chairman coincided with the end of the 9000's troubles. Indeed, within two months of his assumption of the chair, Texas Instruments, who only a year earlier had complained bitterly about their problems with the 9000, awarded ESI their coveted Texas Instruments Supplier Excellence Award. Almost everywhere Bolender looked, there were early signs that things had bottomed out: losses were on the decline; while still not on the increase, orders were flattening out; margins were paper thin, but increased controls and cost-cutting would produce a projected profit of $6 million in fiscal 1993. In the same way that Franklin D. Roosevelt benefited from the bitter policies of his predecessor Herbert Hoover, there was a degree to which Dave Bolender and the next CEO at ESI would end up benefiting from the struggles of the Porter-Ellsworth years.

In January 1992 the board authorized its new chairman to mount a search for a new president/CEO. The attitude Bolender took into the search was critical, since the message he ultimately communicated to candidates was one of excitement and possibility, not panic and despair. In short, Bolender conceived of ESI as a start-up company:

> The underlying fundamentals [of the company] were solid. I said to myself in '92, "you know, if I were starting up a company and I could get this kind of balance sheet, with this kind of distribution system and this kind of sales force, and this kind of engineering talent... there are people who would kill for that kind of stuff."

Bolender's first challenge was to insure continuity in financial management. Ken Olsen, who had succeeded Dean Finley, had done excellent work installing new financial controls. In January 1992, Olsen engaged the consulting services of a friend, an experienced financial hand Barry Harmon, who assisted Olsen in his reform of internal control systems. A native of Seattle, with accounting and banking experience in New York, Harmon was back in Seattle and looking for opportunities in the Northwest. Harmon's arrival at ESI, at such a low point in the company's history, made a lasting impression on him:

> I'll never forget the first day working here. The company had a tradition of having employee meetings regularly, and I just happened to show up for the quarterly meeting. So there were probably four hundred people or so, maybe three hundred and fifty, gathered in the gymnasium [of Bldg. IX] down the street, where Taco Bell is now. And Ken gave a presentation about our financial results that included a big layoff and very poor financial performance. There were four hundred long faces. I think people's sense of reality had been obscured so much that this was all a big shock to them at that time. It was the first part of February of 1992, and it felt like a group of people that literally had bombs thrown on them.
>
> Ken announced that I was going to join on a more or less temporary basis and what my background was and asked me to stand up. You know, the natural thing that most people do in that circumstance is that they at least welcome the person. I'll never forget looking out and seeing all those empty faces. I mean, it was definitely a group of people who were beleaguered.

Once Dave Bolender began as Board Chairman, good things began to happen. Among the earliest blessings was the Supplier Excellence Award Texas Instruments bestowed on ESI in March 1992, just two months after Bolender assumed the Chairman's gavel. Only a year previous, Texas Instruments had complained bitterly about the glitches in the Model 9000. At last, those days were over.

Then one young guy from the shipping department came up to me after the meeting and sort of apologized for everyone's lack of demeanor, shall we say. And he said, "You know, you can't blame these people, they're just really going through a difficult time," and shook my hand and said, "I'm glad you're here."

Harmon had experience managing difficult finances, having earlier helped shepherd Northwest Pipe and Casing through difficult times in 1983. For Harmon, ESI's most pressing problem was managing its cash-flow crisis as the company began to bottom out. "We were skating on very thin ice," he said years later.

By the summer of 1992 ESI's accountant, Arthur Andersen & Co. demanded answers. "I had to convince them that ESI had the resources and the where-with-all to have what accountants call 'the ability to continue in existence,' which translated means 'to survive.'" It was a close call, but Harmon convinced Arthur Andersen, and in the process laid the basis for an extension of ESI's line of credit with the Banc Nationale de Paris, the only remaining bank willing to loan money to the company. "We never used it," Harmon was quick to point out, "but getting the commitment for that loan was very important.... After that, I think the board kind of felt, 'Oh! We will survive.'"

That spring, Ken Olsen began to explore opportunities elsewhere. As Olsen disengaged from ESI, Harmon was a natural candidate to move into the position of chief financial officer. Seeing the finances of the company in increasingly good hands, Bolender could then go on the offensive in the search for president/CEO. During that spring the company's search turned up a number of candidates. One of the most promising, however, seemed already to have his hands full. But Dave Bolender was persistent.

Don VanLuvanee

Young, cerebral, an engineer by training, and an instinctive manager, Don VanLuvanee, came to ESI as President late in the summer of 1992. He had his work cut out for him. Indeed, some investors – and even Board members – feared ESI's days were numbered.

Among those whose names came to Dave Bolender's attention, was that of Don VanLuvanee, at the time the CEO of Mechanical Technology, Inc., a small company in Albany, New York. The path that brought Don together with Dave in the winter of 1992 for conversations about the future of ESI was a circuitous one. Save for World War II, Don VanLuvanee would no doubt be a native Upstate New Yorker. But on the 3rd of July 1944, when Don was born, military service had taken the VanLuvanees to Neosho, Missouri, to Camp Crowder. Before the war, the senior VanLuvanee had worked for IBM, and so when his tour of duty was over at the end of the war and he came back from the Pacific, he returned with his family to Endicott, New York, and to IBM. Once Don and his siblings were in school, his mother also worked at IBM. On the side, Don's dad ran a TV repair business, and he recalled living in a family "where if something broke, you fixed it — you tried your damndest to fix it. So I grew up tinkering with stuff." This home-grown combination of technical curiosity and entrepreneurship would come to serve Don in good stead.

As an "IBM kid," Don VanLuvanee was eligible for the Watson Memorial Merit Scholarship, a competitive scholarship program open to sons and daughters of IBM employees. These were the post-Sputnik days and in Upstate New York IBM, Kodak, GE, Corning and other scientifically-based companies all pitched in to enrich the sciences in high schools throughout the area. With a strong high school science background, and a Watson Scholarship under his arm, in 1962, VanLuvanee headed to Troy,

New York, to Rensselear Polytechnic Institute (RPI), along with Cal Tech and MIT, one of the nation's three leading technical colleges. Armed with an electrical engineering degree, Don faced the dreaded fork in the road: graduate school or industry? Graduate school won out. But, no, in the end, industry won out. The prospect of applied work just seemed more stimulating, and in 1972, Masters Degree in hand, he took a position with Texas Instruments.

The timing was hardly auspicious; the Seventies were lean years. VanLuvanee was with Texas Instruments for eight years, often working on projects that, after twenty-five years, "are still not public." Recruited away from TI in 1980, Don briefly tried his hand in a medical instruments division of Syntex. Quickly discovering that he missed high technology pace (as opposed to the regulatory pace of medical devices), VanLuvanee joined Kulicke and Soffa as vice-president for research and development. K&S was a leading manufacturer of wire bonders and by the mid-Eighties began to move into all areas of semi-conductor assembly. Within a year VanLuvanee assumed responsibility for all K&S's domestic operations and by 1984 had become president and chief operating officer. Despite being a public company, Kulicke & Soffa had not yet emerged from the shadow of its founders. Yearning for the challenge of leading a truly public company, VanLuvanee left K&S in 1990 to tackle a succession of short, sharp business challenges while searching for the presidency he really desired. Briefly, as president of a U.S. branch of the Liechtenstein-based company, Balzers, he helped the parent company sell off their semi-conductor equipment operation to Sony. Then, calling on his experience in the environment of K&S, VanLuvanee worked for a year at Mechanical Technology, Inc.(MTI), in Albany, New York, a thirty-year old company whose board had just taken control from the original founder and had brought Don on board to turn the company around. MTI was out of money, and it fell to VanLuvanee to keep MTI's creditors at bay long enough to turn things around. It was Don's good fortune to have at hand a young man on the MTI team, Joe Reinhart, who had been with MTI for several years, who understood the business, and who had extensive background in investment research, banking and finance. Together, as Reinhart recalled, the two began to restructure the company's debt:

> We worked very closely to maintain as good as possible banking relationships, [since] at that time we were in default of about $20 million in bank debt.... I remember long sessions with bank loan officers and more importantly bank work-out loan officers, where we helped them try to believe that they should have faith in us and our ability to get them their money back.

Within a year, the two had restructured Mechanical Technology's debt. They negotiated the sale of 49% of MTI to a new shareholder that was willing to recapitalize the company. And in the process, Dave Bolender heard about the dynamic turnaround at MTI and its equally dynamic president.

Beginning in January 1992, Bolender contacted Don VanLuvanee. The two men had numerous conversations over the next three months. In May Don signed on. "So, for awhile, I was the CEO of two public companies, MTI in Albany, New York, and ESI in Portland Oregon," VanLuvanee would later recall. "So I learned that you literally can make three meetings, two on one coast and one on the other coast, flying the red-eye back and forth. But if you wanted to change your clothes in the restrooms at that time at Albany County Airport, there wasn't enough room!"

Sorting Things Out

Shuttling between coasts, VanLuvanee wrapped things up at Mechanical Technology, while meeting regularly with Bolender and senior managers at ESI. It was crucial that both Bolender and VanLuvanee were on the same page – Dave would manage the board, Don would manage the company. Neither task was easy. One thing was clear, however: both Bolender and VanLuvanee enjoyed the support and encouragement of Doug Strain. For generations, the historical landscape has been littered with the ruins of companies that have not survived the transition from founder to successors. Often, the children of founders lack the skill, the drive and the leadership abilities of their forebear. Such was not the case with ESI, since no one in the Strain family wanted to continue in the business. One thing stood out, though. Doug, Dave and Don all shared the same underlying commitment to quality, service, and an egalitarian working environment. The three also concurred that for ESI to survive, management and the board had to focus on the bottom line. Finally, working closely together, the three men structured Doug Strain's withdrawal from the day-to-day operations of the company, allowing him the latitude of a long-postponed retirement while remaining Vice-Chairman of the Board of Directors.

Upon his arrival in the late summer of 1992, VanLuvanee found employee morale "surprisingly, not bad." But there was a surreal quality that he immediately recognized: even though many employees believed that ESI might indeed go out of business, few actually seemed to believe that her or his job would cease to exist. The initial period of a new executive officer is always a delicate moment. Will the new leader begin to change the organization immediately? Or will there be an interval during which the new person studies the organization, learning the strengths and weakness of its culture? For the first few months, Don spent his time exploring the company, listening in meetings and assessing the situation. What few could know at that stage, however, was that Don VanLuvanee already understood a key component of ESI's culture.

Although Don no doubt used ESI "boxes," bridges and decade resistors, at Rensselaer, and in graduate school, his first conscious encounter with ESI equipment came at Texas Instruments as he was working on a problem with remote control circuit breakers for the Lockheed L-1011. "It was probably a Model 20 trimmer in the mid-Seventies." At TI, Don's group was part of a "technology stretching team... doing some work using lasers as a potential processing instrument." As part of his research, he saw not only ESI's machine, but those of Chicago Laser as well:

> So I started out to go and visit companies, you know, a nondisclosure and here's what we're trying to do. Chicago Laser was easy to work with. I went and spent a day, and we tried some things. I can remember that ESI was more difficult....
>
> The issue was an application that had the potential to be used in every integrated circuit that TI made, and they were number one in the business at that time... Clearly ESI had a leg up, because I think they had good equipment, but you know I got what I needed out of Chicago Laser.... [ESI had] the sense that if only our customers were smart enough, they would appreciate how good we are.... But ESI was not alone in this, because the whole equipment industry certainly grew up this way – a focus on features and neat stuff, as opposed to what do customers need to be successful.

Although VanLuvanee moved on, having gotten what he needed from Chicago Laser, somewhere in the back of his mind remained the thought that ESI needed to work on its marketing and positioning with customers.

During VanLuvanee's "walkabout," as he got to know ESI during his first few months, he began to sense that the structure of things on paper, "the virtual structure," as he came to call it, and the real management structure were "totally misaligned." And the fulcrum of the misalignment was the customer:

> I remember coming in. We had the classic "Total Quality" type problem solving, and it wasn't bad except nowhere in this equation was the word "customer" ever mentioned. We even had our own internal Malcolm Baldridge score, but my simple understanding of Malcolm Baldridge is that with zero customer input, the maximum score [you can get] is zero.

In group meetings, and one-on-one, the challenge went out: "Stop talking about the quality function, quality is everyone's job. Don't concentrate on internal frictions, look outside to our customers and our competitors to see how we can serve our customers better than our competitors."

Gradually, a cultural shift began at ESI. At base, this shift was from an essentially passive to an active strategic vision. Previously, ESI had come to believe, in effect, that "if we build it they will come." In its place emerged a new strategic vision: determine ESI's core businesses, consolidate those positions, and compete.

Building a Team

Arriving as he did at a low moment in ESI's fortunes, VanLuvanee inherited austerity measures that included pay and hiring freezes, departmental budget cuts, and the suspension of some employee benefits programs. As a clear signal that these sacrifices were not to be born by line employees alone, in September of 1992 executive bonuses and incentives were also suspended, to be paid only if the company met its business objectives and individuals met or exceeded their goals. Such austere fiscal measures were not only called for, but carried immense symbolic value. Every bit as vivid was the continued personnel turnover that attended the changing of the guard at ESI. What began with the resignation of Mike Ellsworth as president, and board members Shaw and Elorriaga, continued before VanLuvanee arrived. Ken Olsen departed, to be replaced by Barry Harmon, acting in a consulting role. Shortly thereafter, the head of Portland manufacturing and operations, Chris Nawrocki, left, and was replaced by Don Smith. As Don VanLuvanee arrived, changes continued. They had been in the offing at Palomar for some time, and with the resignation of Jim Currier, the position of Vice-President/ General Manager of Palomar was filled by Mark Klug.

One of the great strengths of the Paul Lintner years was the team that Paul put together to run ESI. Paul had inherited some; he recruited others. Likewise, Don VanLuvanee spent considerable time and effort assembling a team that could bring ESI back to its position as industry leader. By his own admission, Don had the great good fortune to inherit Barry Harmon as his financial right-hand man. Well, not exactly inherit, since Harmon was technically only consulting with ESI when Don arrived. "I went out after Barry," Don says with a grin. "The more I knew about him, the more I recruited him;

As he put his new team together, VanLuvanee built his team on the cornerstone of Barry Harmon's financial management. Barry was Don's "indispensable" right hand, whose integrity and fiscal savvy allowed VanLuvanee to concentrate on other matters.

I unleashed an army of arm-twisters." Eventually, Harmon succumbed: "Barry came in and he says, 'I surrender. You got everybody I know in the Portland area asking me what's wrong with me!' And he agreed to join as CFO." One thing Don particularly liked was Barry's straight talk. In fact, while Harmon's blunt assessment of ESI during the search process had been enough to make Dave Bolender blanch, Don liked what he saw: "Here's a guy who was a straight shooter, articulate, had a sense of business, not just accounting, carried himself like a senior officer, which I think is part of a leader's job, and people have a right to expect that." The two worked overtime to stabilize ESI's finances. This included a series of in-house meetings with all employees – "in-house CFO training" Don would call it – to open everyone's eyes to why the company's stock had hit a low of $2.35 in the fourth quarter of fiscal 1992. Within a year of Don's arrival, Barry could announce that ESI's liquidity was the best it had been in the past five years.

The chief financial officer is a crucial member of a management team, and Barry Harmon's presence allowed VanLuvanee to concentrate on other positions. Even as he began to summon outside talent, some from colleagues he had known previously, some unknown until then, Don also had the good fortune to be able to call on a few old hands. Although scarred by countless wars over competing technologies, and one of the leading mutineers, Senior Vice President for Research and Development Ed Swenson nevertheless remained a strong voice within ESI for the development of new technologies. And while the many battles had taken their toll on Ed over the years, his passion for technology and his ability to articulate a vision for the company's future remained an asset VanLuvanee was determined to husband. As Don restructured his management team, Ed remained a very significant voice as Senior Vice President.

In addition to Barry Harmon and Ed Swenson, another veteran soon became an indispensable member of the VanLuvanee team: Larry Rapp. Larry Rapp was born in 1940 in Baker, Oregon. Graduating from Baker High School in 1958, he headed for Klamath Falls and Oregon Technical Institute (later Oregon Institute of Technology). At the height of the Cold War, Rapp was recruited by a Chicago electronics firm, Hallicrafters, where he worked testing radar jammers. After three years Rapp moved to Motorola's military and aerospace engineering center in Chicago. In the fall of 1965, Larry attended the NEC electronics show at McCormick Place in Chicago. He had the assignment of buying a capacitance bridge for the project he was working on at the time at Motorola. That meant he went back and forth from the GenRad booth to the ESI booth. Eventually, he struck up a conversation with a man at the ESI booth. The man asked him where he was from and where he went to school. "Why are you in Chicago?" the man asked. "Because there are no jobs in Oregon," Rapp replied. They continued to talk; the man was interested in Rapp's experience with semiconductors, since ESI was still using vacuum tubes, but planned on using semiconductors in their new meter calibrator. Would Larry be interested in coming out to ESI? "I said I'd be interested, but I thought at the time he was just trying to sell me the capacitance bridge."

The man was Doug Strain. "He never told me until I was leaving the booth, after he talked to me about a job, and he handed me his card that he was the president and chairman." He took Larry's name and address, and "about three weeks later a fellow named Harold Lawson, who was then chief engineer at ESI, called me and wanted to know when I was coming to work for them!" Over the years Rapp worked as a technician and engineer on a number of projects. Eventually Charlie Davis moved Larry into his operation. Once Dean Finley arrived, Larry found himself doing special projects for Finley. It might be working on the details of the profit sharing trust, or the mechanics of selling a piece of land ESI owned, or making site visits to ESI's European operations, all in his capacity as assistant secretary-treasurer. And it was Rapp who had to pick up the pieces following Stenger's resignation in 1987.

At the same time, during the Eighties, Rapp became ESI's specialist in a variety of government regulations. While lasers were regulated by the Food and Drug Administration, elsewhere there were elaborate export regulations overseen by agencies as disparate as the Department of Commerce and the Department of Defense. Larry logged weeks at a time in Washington, D.C. as ESI's chief lobbyist and facilitator. Because so much of ESI's business in the Eighties was overseas — at times up to seventy percent — and because the normal turn-around time on export licenses was upwards of six months, Rapp would often personally carry applications throughout Washington's bureaucratic maze. Often enlisting the help of Oregon's Congressional delegation, in particular Mark Hatfield and Les AuCoin, Rapp would personally camp out in the office of the official whose signature he needed next. "I made sure I took this one guy out to lunch at least eight to ten times a month. He had this little tiny office, and stacks of applications several feet high all over. I'd go in and sort through the piles, and put ours at the top of the stack."

While the luster of Larry Rapp's work went unnoticed by many at ESI, those close to him — Dean Finley, Charlie Davis, Mike Ellsworth — understood the importance of his contributions. Of those contributions, none was more indicative of his grit and thoroughness than his work on precursor to ESI's great era of acquisitions: Ballantine.

Throughout the late 1980's and the 1990's, one of ESI's "go-to guys" was Larry Rapp. Not only did Larry serve as Dean Finley's right-hand man when it came to fixing organizational and inventory problems at ESI GmbH and the liquidation of the Ballantine subsidiary, at the same time he took over from Charlie Davis as ESI's chief lobbyist in Washington. Here, in 1985, Davis (right) and Rapp (left) following a meeting with Oregon's senior Senator, Bob Packwood.

Lessons Learned

By virtually any measure, ESI's first acquisition — Palomar Systems and Machines in 1982 — was a success. A closer marriage of the technologies of ESI and Palomar was always possible, and even skeptics were convinced by the late Eighties, when Palomar's sales helped keep ESI afloat. Despite the increasingly unfavorable business climate of the Eighties, the evident successes of Palomar and ESI's overseas subsidiaries convinced senior management at ESI to keep an eye out for other possible acquisition targets. Thus, a spirit prevailed in which an acquisition, if promising, would receive due consideration. And it was in this spirit that in 1986, just before the market downturn, ESI acquired Metoramic Sciences, Inc. (MSI). MSI produced materials for the multi-layer ceramic capacitor industry, and was a ideal addition to ESI's Component Materials and Equipment Division, where on-going efforts focused on refining equipment for the passive components market.

The MSI acquisition was modest and, as with Palomar, widely considered a shrewd move. These successes were encouraging. By 1988, as the systems business hit the skids, it made perfect sense to look again at ESI's original business: instruments. Perhaps the time was right for ESI to attempt to consolidate its position in the instrument business through the acquisition of smaller, struggling instrument companies, and thus insure the future of instruments at ESI. The company that caught ESI's eye was the privately-held

Ballantine Laboratories, in Boonton, New Jersey. One of the country's oldest instrument companies, Ballantine was founded in 1927. Ballantine's product line spanned the gamut from throat microphones for Air Force pilots, to meter calibrators for the Navy. If there was a common thread that ran through Ballantine's business, it was government contracts, and as government contracts had long been a staple of ESI's instrument business, this was no problem. Negotiations began in 1988, and in the spring of 1989 ESI acquired Ballantine Labs.

From the beginning, the Ballantine venture was a mistake. Not only was much of the Ballantine line outmoded, they never did complete their contract with the Navy for meter calibrators. Worse yet, it soon became apparent that Ballantine was not able to collect on their outstanding government contracts, since they had failed to file the proper paperwork. Within a year Ellsworth and company decided that Ballanatine had to go. Finley dispatched Larry Rapp back to Boonton to sort out the mess and get Ballantine sold. Rapp located Joanne Sunnarborg while she was on vacation. Sunnarborg had become ESI's most skilled government contracts manager, and together Rapp and Sunnarborg corralled Ballantine's government accounts, redid the paperwork and resubmitted the bills to Washington for payment:

> Joanne was able to collect most of this money by redoing all the paperwork and working with the government. She saved us hundreds of thousands of dollars.
> She was actually on vacation back East, and somebody told me about it. I asked her to come over… She went through and cleaned up everything. It was unbelievable. Super.

Ballantine was an expensive lesson. Selling Ballantine turned out to be far more difficult than Rapp had figured. The sins of an earlier generation were visited on ESI, when the State of New Jersey required ESI to undertake an environmental clean-up of the Ballantine property before it could be sold. Ultimately, in 1990, ESI did sell Ballantine, at a substantial loss.

In retrospect, however, some good did come from the Ballantine fiasco. In fact, ESI learned two crucial lessons. Bloodied but unbowed, a chastened ESI would, in future, dramatically improve its research and due-diligence prior to any acquisition. Second, and perhaps more significant, ESI's experience with Ballantine Labs bore with it an unwelcome but unavoidable message. The general failure of Ballantine's instrument line, combined with the painful review of Ballantine's accounts, forced ESI to confront a reality that many at the company had long feared and hoped to postpone: the instrument business was drying up. As the man in the trenches, literally cleaning up the Ballantine mess, Larry Rapp could see clearly that ESI's instrument business was headed toward a dwindling number of private clients, since the aerospace industry was slowing down and the number of standards labs around the world was shrinking. "From there forward, the opportunity to sell instruments was getting down to a few government labs around the world and a few — well essentially Boeing and Airbus, maybe — labs in private industry."

So it was that one of the most painful decisions ESI had to make fell to Dave Bolender and Don VaLuvanee, as they sought in 1993-1994 to lead the board, senior management and the ESI family to consider the future of the instrument business within the larger scope of the strategic vision for the company. Doug Strain was simply the most senior and most prominent proponents of ESI's instrument business. Many, like Joanne Sunnarborg, Chris Beeler, Larry Rapp himself, and others, felt a deep affection for the instruments business. Doug, in particular, was torn. His heart was with instruments, for after all, ESI started out as an instruments company. But as a businessman, his head appreciated reality. And the reality was harsh. As Dave Bolender recalled, Barry Harmon's figures did not lie: "We were not making any money [on instruments]. We were spending an awful lot of time and effort, there was a huge inventory of 50-year-old parts that we were carrying. Inventory turns weren't worth a damn any more because there weren't very many labs any more using bridges." Dave and Don brought Doug into the conversation, fully aware of how painful this might be for Doug, but knowing, too, how deeply Doug was committed to what was best for ESI. The three discussed the numbers, the inventory, how much management time went into the instrument business. "What would you think of selling it?" they asked Doug. The decision was unavoidable, "and when we agreed, Doug really got into it and got behind it. He made a personal [commitment] — he wanted to make sure that the person who got it would take care of the customers and would love it like he loved it and would nurture it like he nurtured it."

The person who met Doug's criteria was a man named Terry Gamble. Doug became aware of Gamble through an old friend, Joe Keithley, of Keithley Instruments. Keithley told Doug about this young man who was putting a company together out of parts of other companies, as they sold off their instrument businesses. He had had the idea when Leeds & Northrup went out of business. So Gamble picked up the L&N calibration line, some of Keithley's line, acquired Gertsch's ratio transformer business, made the connection to ESI, and in the process even took on some of Tektronix' older instruments. Strain and Gamble hit if off; it was clear to Doug that Gamble intended to run a first-rate operation:

> He had the idea that there's still a market for these instruments that were being phased out. If you could find four or five of those 38 million businesses, you could put together a $40 million company.... I guess all of us [ESI, Keithley, Leeds & Nothrup, Genrad, Tektronix] had too much pride in what we were doing to go around and pick up all our competitors. But he didn't, and everyone made him a good deal.

On April 6, 1994 the ESI Board of Directors, in a special telephone conference meeting, approved the sale of the company's "Standards, Calibration and General Instrument (Product) Lines to Tegam, Inc.," closing the book on ESI's original product line. In the end, even Strain himself felt good about the company's decision, since he knew very well the world had changed:

> When we started, you could see a lot of reason when the international labs were in disagreement by say a tenth of a percent or more in fundamental measurements. One percent sometimes. You couldn't do good physics; you couldn't do good international engineering if you had that much disagreement in your fundamentals, because a lot of these things have to be accurate to one-thousandth of one-percent. So until we got all those measurements pinned down to one part per million, which is where they are now, you couldn't really be satisfied.
>
> Once you got there, to one part per million, then the practical impact on the art was minimal. Once you get there, why push it further? Who needs it?
>
> The one part per million barrier was a nice drive, you know, to move it from one-tenth of a percent to one part per million... but once we got there,

it's kind of like everything else, you know. So vacuum tubes went out, too, and they just disappear, and new things come on. I'm glad we made the transition.

Acquiring the Future

Even as ESI internalized the most painful lesson from the Ballantine episode, ultimately divesting itself of its instrument business, the other lesson – research and due diligence – took root. Even before Don VanLuvanee arrived, ESI ventured into a new acquisition. This time, however, things were different. Different factors drove the next acquisition, and ESI was at the right place at the right time.

By the end of the Eighties, ESI's memory-repair line, including the 9000 Series, used a vision subsystem built for ESI by Cognex. "Vision," as it pertains to laser trimming and memory repair, involves mapping the circuit board or the silicon wafer being trimmed or repaired. The mapped data are entered into a specialized computer that can read video signals from a picture of the circuit board or wafer, analyze the data signals and then locate a precise micro-spot on the circuit board or wafer. All of this is automated and done at very high speed. In short, "vision" constantly identifies points of reference, allowing the mechanisms controlling the laser to align swiftly and precisely so the laser can do its work at a particular spot on the material.

In 1991 ESI learned that a little company in Corvallis, Oregon, Intelledex, was about to go under. What might have been no more than a footnote in the *Business Journal* was of real interest to ESI, since Intelledex produced vision systems. Eventually, as ESI looked into it, the Intelledex vision system was indeed superior to the system ESI was buying from Cognex. The receivership in the Intelledex bankruptcy fell to the First Interstate Bank. The timing was terrific; the bank could hardly wait to get Intelledex off their books and ESI was there with a proposal. The deal included facilities and office equipment that ESI was able to sell, covering much of the cost of the deal. The vision project was relocated from Corvallis to Willsonville, and ultimately to Beaverton, eventually allowing ESI to develop its own vision systems without Cognex. In 1991 and 1992, however, as leadership changes dominated the company's immediate horizon, little attention was paid to the new vision operation. Nevertheless, the acquisition of Intelledex and its vision component planted a seed. Whether it would germinate remained to be seen.

For ESI's embryonic foray into vision to bear fruit would take a different kind of "vision," a strategic vision of the company's potential and a willingness to think differently about how ESI should grow. One of the things that virtually everyone agreed on was that Don VanLuvanee brought a different kind of strategic vision to the table. His was a much more aggressive, market-driven view. During his first year, VanLuvanee challenged, pushed, pulled and challenged again those around him to think more competitively. By the winter of 1993-1994, one could sense a change. Ed Swenson had already begun to articulate new opportunities in micromachining, interconnect systems, link-processing and new trimming technologies. The Intelledex seed began to open, as Dave McCullough's vision team doubled the performance of their latest vision system at a production cost reduction of 25%. That April ESI lightened its load with the sale of the instruments line. No better sign of the gathering momentum of the new ESI could be found than in the third-quarter high in ESI shares of $15.50, a 564% jump in just two years from the fourth-quarter low of $2.35 in 1992.

Hard on the heals of the sale of the instruments line, VanLuvanee, Harmon and Rapp unveiled a bold new initiative: the acquisition of ESI's chief laser systems competitor, Chicago Laser Systems, Inc. (CLS). Founded in 1976, Chicago Laser Systems became the second largest supplier of laser systems for fine tuning electric circuits. Through aggressive marketing, particularly overseas, CLS proved a nettlesome competitor. Smaller than ESI, privately held, CLS had an agility that ESI found frustrating. When he was at Texas Instruments, Don VanLuvanee had seen personally what that meant.

In retrospect, the timing of the CLS acquisition could not have been better. Coming as it did within days of the sale of ESI's instrument business, the CLS acquisition sent a powerful message both internally and externally. Internally, it had powerful impact on morale, demonstrating to the ESI family that the company had no intention of resting on its laurels. It would grow in the most dynamic areas of its core strength, and this growth would include acquiring competitors and key technologies. To the external community, ESI's acquisition of CLS clearly signaled ESI's new willingness to compete at any level. The fact that ESI, a mere eight financial quarters from the precipice in the spring of 1992, could acquire CLS was a powerful tonic to the company itself, and a breathtaking signal to the industry. To shareholders, and potential investors, it demonstrated another factor in ESI's cultural shift: a willingness to be decisive when it came to cutting costs, trimming operations and consolidating assets. Under Barry Harmon's guidance ESI consolidated its financial position by selling off assets that no longer benefited the company, including the schoolhouse and a cluster of properties adjacent to ESI's campus in Science Park. With a solid bottom line, ESI could finance a stock purchase of Chicago Laser Systems, sending a message of fiscal health to the industry and the investment community that was impossible to miss.

By 1995 the electronics market was a radically different place than it had been only three years before. Foreign markets had picked up dramatically, providing fully 55% of ESI's business. Domestically, the increasing computerization of automobile systems, the sudden emergence of wireless telecommunications and pc's everywhere, rekindled markets that for some time had lain dormant. Globally, the demand for the new 16 megabit dynamic random access memory (DRAM) chips meant fresh demand for ESI's memory repair systems. The view from Science Park looked good.

Respected and Feared

In their annual report to shareholders in 1994, Dave Bolender and Don VanLuvanee minced few words in announcing ESI's future course: "We intend to be the most respected supplier and the most feared competitor in the markets we serve." This single sentence summed up the basis of ESI's strategic vision. Building on the continuity of the respect ESI had earned over forty years of setting the standard for precision measurement instruments and laser systems, ESI would no longer simply build the better mousetrap and wait for people to come to Portland, ESI would lead the battle in the marketplace.

The CLS acquisition opened a new chapter in ESI's history. From that point on, acquisitions came with dizzying rapidity, and with the targeted precision of ESI's own

As Harmon and VanLuvanee put ESI's fiscal house in order, Don brought Joe Reinhart to ESI. Reinhart's skill as an investment analyst, and his ability to "think outside the box," was the final element in what became ESI's strategic acquisition team. Together, the three took ESI into new ventures in vision, packaging and micro-drilling, opening new markets and inviting new technologies that will carry ESI into the next century.

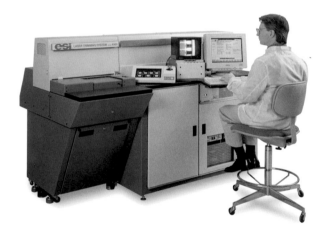

lasers. Even as the company integrated CLS into its operations, ESI set out to absorb its next laser competitor, XRL, Inc., of Canton, Massachusetts. Founded in 1984, XRL manufactured laser systems specifically aimed at improving the yields in the DRAMs, as well as SRAMs, or static random access memory. In the summer of 1995, ESI acquired XRL. XRL was a perfect strategic fit for ESI, since it gave the company a low-end memory repair line to deal with General Scanning, ESI's major competitor at that end of the market. To the delight of folks at ESI, the engineering talent at XRL proved to be a great asset, particularly with respect to XRL's galvanometer-based systems. While most of XRL's manufacturing relocated to Portland, ESI chose to maintain XRL's laboratory in Canton, where roughly two dozen engineers, connected by teleconferencing to Beaverton, work on parts of ESI's newest laser systems.

As the details of the XRL acquisition crystallized, it became clear that ESI would have its first $100 million sales year. The company's success was reflected not only in sales figures, but in rapidly increasing gross margins, net income per share, and share price, which closed fiscal 1995's forth quarter at $24.37 per share. Most satisfying to Harmon was the reduction of debt as a percentage of capitalization, a figure that stood at 19.3% in 1992 and had fallen to 0.0% in 1995. Such success occasioned salary adjustments at all levels within the company, enabling ESI to insure that its most vital asset, its human capital, was compensated at competitive levels.

In 1993 VanLuvanee had made an acquisition of a different sort, and by 1995 Don had identified the final member of what has come to be widely regarded as perhaps the industry's most gifted acquisitions team. In May of 1993, Joe Reinhart arrived at ESI. Joe and Don had worked together at Mechanical Technology, and when Don left to come to ESI the two remained in contact. Don brought Joe out as Director of Communications, with the specific assignment of tackling investor and shareholder communications. Within a very short period it became apparent, however, that Reinhart's energy and analytical skill equipped him for a far more important role. Reinhart complemented Harmon in ways that Barry was quick to acknowledge:

> Joe is very creative. He thinks about things that I don't think anyone else around the company can connect, and he does it by being involved in a lot of sporadic activities that don't necessarily have a connection. He's able to think through his experiences and say, "Well, what about this?" His biggest contribution is his ability to develop very unique ideas about what we should be doing or what we could be doing.

With VanLuvanee's overall strategic vision of turning ESI into a dominant competitor, with Barry Harmon's financial savvy and Joe Reinhart's creative insights, ESI fashioned a laser-sharp precision instrument for tracking down, acquiring and developing new opportunities.

ESI to the Fifth Power

As the historian approaches the present, the clarity with which events present themselves first begins to dim, then to blur, and finally to disappear altogether. Seldom does the historian experience the rush of events so swiftly as in high technology, where the speed of data transmission itself seems to accelerate exponentially every few years. Thus, the historian's perspective becomes less certain, more speculative, as we approach 1999.

What can be said with certainty is that within the past four years ESI has remade itself yet again. Since 1995 ESI has moved to solidify its five core businesses. In the process, from the board room to the engineer's bench, from marketing to manufacturing to maintenance, ESI has taken on a new look. No longer an instruments company, ESI has established five core businesses: memory yield products; circuit fine tuning products ceramic capacitor manufacturing equipment; advanced electronic packaging products; and vision products. The five businesses are interlocking, each with technology that overlaps and compliments its partners.

In rapid succession, between September 1995 and early 1999, the Harmon, Reinhart, VanLuvanee team led ESI in the acquisition of Cybernetic Systems, Applied Intelligent Systems, Inc. (AISI), Dynamotion Corporation, ChipStar, Inc., Testec, Inc. and MicroVision, Corp. The combined effect of these acquisitions has been to place ESI in an increasingly competitive position in the markets the company has chosen to develop. Acquired in January 1996, Cybernetic Systems expanded ESI's vision development into electronic assembly. Harmon, Reinhart, and VanLuvanee next zeroed in on Dynamotion Corp., in June 1997. Dynamotion was a leading supplier of mechanical drilling products for the advanced electronic packaging industry. The acquisition of Dynamotion fit well with ESI's entry into the laser drilling field, expanding ESI's market to the complete range of micro-via drilling for advanced electronic packaging. Then, catching their second wind, in that same month ESI's team announced the acquisition of ChipStar, Inc, a leader in the design and manufacture of capacitor termination equipment. Started by the same Denver Braden who had founded Palomar, ChipStar's products fit perfectly with those of Palomar Systems Division's capacitor production equipment. A mere five months later, in December 1997, ESI acquired Applied Intelligent Systems, a major supplier of vision equipment. Pausing to catch their breath, for the next eighteen months ESI's target acquisition radar swept the horizon. Finally, in December 1998 and January 1999, came two new acquisitions: Testec, Inc. and MicroVision. Testec, founded by an old ESI hand, Josef Baumann, manufactured specialized electrical test equipment for the newest and most sophisticated passive components, and was an ideal addition to the Palomar Systems Division. MicroVision was a premier manufacturer of machine-based process inspection and characterization equipment, operating on circuits in both the wafer and the finished packaged state. Along with the technology benefits for ESI's vision development, MicroVision, which produces turnkey systems to a wide spectrum of customers, promises to expand ESI's vision market dramatically.

Through its acquisitions ESI has compounded its assets many times over, in human terms, in technology and in markets. Since 1992 ESI's steadily improving performance has been reflected in many ways. Acquisitions are just one way in which the reversal in the company's fortunes can be measured. Shareholder return on investment, indeed investor confidence, has been richly rewarded. ESI's share price and return on investment have kept pace with its expansion. It is no accident, then, that the annual increase in ESI's research and development expenditures have led to a superior product line. In each of ESI's five core businesses, ESI's products lead the industry. In the semiconductor industry, ESI's Model 9350 Memory Yield Improvement System utilizes a 1.321 micron laser to deliver higher energy with less substrate damage in cutting metal links used in

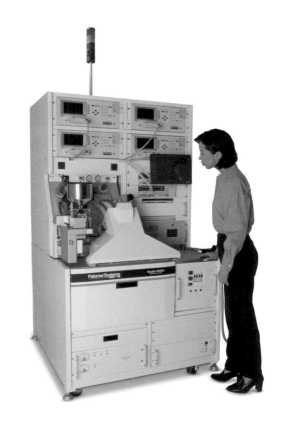

As ESI closes out the Century by celebrating its 55th year, a product line positioned to take ESI into the 21st Century numbers industry leaders in every key sector: (upper left) the Model 9350 Memory Yield Improvement System; (lower left) the Model 4300 Laser Trimming System; (upper right) the Model 3300 Multi-Function Chip Capacitor; and (lower right) the Model 5200 Laser Drilling System.

advanced 16, 64 and 256 megabit memory chips. In circuit fine tuning, ESI has led the industry for a quarter of a century. ESI's Laser Trimmer line includes five different models offering a range of beam-positioning resolution, including the Model 4300 at 2.5 microns. Within the telecommunications, automotive and consumer electronics industries, ESI's customers include Delco, Ericsson, Ford, IBM, Motorola, Nippon-Denso, Siemens and Kyocera. In ceramic capacitor manufacturing equipment, ESI Palomar's Model 3300 Multi-function Chip Capacitor Tester offers the unparalleled throughput of 180,000 parts per hour favored by surface mount ceramic capacitor manufacturers the world over. Advanced electronic packaging equipment is led by ESI's Model 5200 Micro-via Laser Drilling System, which can process single or multi-layered laminated materials at rates up to 10,000 vias per minute, using ESI's proprietary, solid-state, ultra-violet laser and beam-positioning technology. Dynamotion's Model Six-Pak computer-controlled mechanical drilling system sold to printed circuit board (PCB) and semiconductor package manufacturers, can drill holes as small as .004 inches in diameter. Dynamotion's computer-controlled routers are also favorites of PCB manufacturers. Finally, ESI's machine vision line combines advanced computer technology, proprietary software and optical equipment to reduce application development time and provide machine vision inspection that facilitates quality and fast throughput. Not only does ESI machine vision enhance ESI's own products, ESI machine vision provides original equipment manufacturers with a wide variety of solutions for automated process control and visual inspection for customers that include Canon, IBM, Kulicke and Soffa, Lucent Technologies, Motorola, Siemens and Universal Instruments.

In 1998 ESI employed 900 people. What had begun in 1949 with fewer than a dozen people had grown by 1985 to a company of more than 1100. In 1985, those 1100 "ESIers" generated $84.1 million in net sales, and a net income of $8.6 million. Shareholder equity was $44.2 million and the company had $5.4 million in long-term debt. In 1998, what immediately strikes the visitor is that a company with such market presence, whose products are known the world over, is so lean. Whereas in 1985, those 1100 employees generated $76,454 of sales per person, for a net income of $7,818 per employee, in 1998, ESI recorded net sales of $229.6 million, and net income of $27.8 million. Shareholder equity stood at $182.3 million and long-term debt at $0.0. Those 900 "ESIers" of 1998, by comparison to their 1100 predecessors in 1985, generated a remarkable $255,111 sales per person, for a net income of $30,889 per employee.

In the final analysis, the modest company that took its cue from its equally modest founder, Doug Strain, has risen like a phoenix from its crises. Almost killed by fire in 1957, brought low by the death of Paul Lintner in 1984, drained by the trauma of a culture war in 1987, exhausted by external and internal forces virtually to the point of extinction by 1992, today's ESI is a different place. The new ESI has become more "respected" than "feared," since, after all, "competition" compels by its very nature an opponent. As one reflects back over half a century, one is gratified that this new competitive spirit that permeates ESI's strategy is built on the firm foundation of ESI's earliest value: **A Passion for Quality**.

ESI has never wavered. **A Passion for Quality** has always meant that ESI has given employees a workplace that guarantees the dignity of work and a respect for each individual. **A Passion for Quality** has meant that from the president on down, no social barrier would separate one from another, and that every employee was encouraged to be a leader, leading by a dedication to the best possible product. **A Passion for Quality** has meant that, as employees, ESI people have shared fairly in the profits, and in the hardships, as the company's fortunes have waxed and waned over the years. **A Passion for Quality** has meant that ESI produced precision instruments and systems of the very highest technical specifications. **A Passion for Quality** has meant that ESI's customers were treated to the highest ethical business practices, and received the finest support and service in the industry. For as Dr. Tony George, retired President of Motorola's Semiconductor Product Sector is fond of saying, "Quality is not a mathematical formula or a process. Quality is what the customer says it is; nothing more, nothing less." **A Passion for Quality** has meant that over the years, ESI, its founders and its leaders, have given unstintingly of their time and resources in the community in hundreds of quiet, generous and meaningful ways. Ultimately, **A Passion for Quality** has meant that within Portland, within Oregon, and within the electronics industry nationally, the name Electro Scientific Industries is synonymous with Leadership. In the end, **A Passion for Quality** at ESI has fulfilled itself: **Quality produces Quality**